Musings on Music: 2

Forthcoming

A Little Book of Poems

And Then? A Perception of the Path of Our Culture

Unexpected Places: Experiencing the Imaginal World

Musings on Music

Bk 2: Philosophy and History

Clement Jewitt, PhD

Greenleaves

Published by Greenleaves, 2023
email: notinototherthanmecj@duck.com

ISBN: 978-0-9930621-2-4

Permissions received for:
Chapter 1—Ch.23 in the book 'A New Renaissance'
Chapters 5 & 6, edited, & Appendix 3—from 'Music & Psyche Journal'

Dedicated to all those who influenced what I have become:

Parents, family, friends, enemies, colleagues, tutors, villains,

spiritual leaders, lovers—welcomed or recoiled from,

all have played a part in moulding my clay.

With much gratitude to my wife Margaret who with

these good friends and colleagues have helped me

create this book: Deirdre Burton, Sarah Verney

and Geoffrey Poole. They have taught me

the inestimable values of friendship.

Contents

Introduction

I am deeply concerned with the one dimensionalization and trivialization of experience [engaged in] by our society, which endangers the capacity to experience individuality and complexity. I deeply believe that listening to music can restore this capacity.   *Jeremy Shapiro*

PUTTING THIS SECOND BOOK TOGETHER I noted that the thoughts in the various essays reach out to, and are simultaneously supported by, aspects of life and culture other than the purely musical. And this is as it should be, for music is not a strictly separate and distinct wedge of our lives as we live them. It is an aspect which is, barring psychological disfunction, a normality, rarely examined as such, just unquestioned, or as I express it in *Music at the Bauhaus*,[1] 'intrinsic to the human psyche'.

Music may sometimes *appear* to have its own niche cordoned off from other parts of our lives, but it is in actuality supported by a number of quite definite knowings, cultural leanings, personal psychologies, and events within a complex, and now for this writer and composer, a quite long life—and that comment necessarily ignores the all too common habit of walking out focussed on a smartphone, or hiding inside headphones, howsoever perceived as a necessity, unconsciously or not, but actually facilitating avoidance of other people, that

---

1   Published in Tempo, No.213., July 2000.

precise indication of our dying culture, avoiding that necessity for the health of soma and psyche, communing with fellow humans.

Hence these idiosyncratic musings jump about somewhat, con-joining various aspects of 'life, the universe and everything' with notions on the beingness of music, internally and externally. And we should notice in passing that music was a necessary and meaningful part of ancient sciences of measurement.

Some chapters are more pointedly focussed, with specific goals, which certainly applies to some historical essays, though even there I make use of a model of flows in the psyche developed by psychotherapist Gareth Hill some 30 to 50 years ago, founded on innovative psychiatrist and psychologist C.G. Jung's findings of contrasexual properties in men and women, a model which I found highly appropriate to track musical movements, paralleling composers' mind flows.[2] Psychology has been one of my in-depth studies, focussing particularly on the work of Jung, which is most obvious in the Jung Club talk, but present perhaps less obviously in other discourses.

This perhaps needs stating, but (the inevitability of the word 'but' arises here) the musics examined, alluded to, looked sideways upon in this book, are largely anything *but* what has always been the natural expression of all people—folk music, so called: the spontaneous breaking into song, or the collective joining in of well known cultural music markers with voice or

2   Hill commented that I was the first to perceive artistic usages

'folk' instrumentation, hymn singing through to indigenous shamanic drumming, aiming maybe at so called altered states.

And there is little consideration of other musics, such as birdsong, or the natural sounds facilitated by moving air, which we looked at briefly in the Introduction to Book 1. No, most of this, with some exceptions, is musings about the curious corners of what is often described as 'Art Music', the Western World applauding itself. The two exceptions are the examinations of ancient musics which are prior to 'Art Music': Chapters 5 and 6, *The archaeology of sounds in ancient sites* and *Hidden faces of ancient Indian song*.

There are two groups dividing the writings,

First there is a short focus under the title **Philosophy,** presenting musings on meaningfulness: a piece on possible futures for the arts, which was a chapter in *A New Renaissance*,[3] and a look at the healing aspects of music. This is followed by a short exposition of Gareth Hill's *Flows in the Psyche*, mentioned above, sufficient for the applications here, its cyclical structural usages appearing as framework in the larger works, particularly in the Jung Club presentation (Ch.4). But not in *Music at the Bauhaus*, originally published in the contemporary music journal *Tempo*, which preceded my delighted discovery of Hill's work.

The chapters on historical investigations occupy the main part of the book. The articles and reviews included which had

---

3   Lorimer & Robinson, eds. 2010

been published elsewhere are edited, at the least to remove textual errors, more to improve elucidation of meanings, and some taken as core thoughts for some expansion.

Following all those there are Appendices: an appreciation of the Journal Time and Mind; a supplement to the major piece on healing musics (Ch.2); together with the second part of a three way discussion with fellow composers

PHILOSOPHY

One

Music and the arts in a possible future

WHEN I WAS CONSIDERING HOW TO APPROACH THIS TOPIC, I drafted an imaginary story of it, as a text deciphered from a strange 'memory stick', found in a wood (perhaps I was in an altered state !) seemingly a documentary gift from a future thoroughly freed from the increasingly manifested and enforced focus on the material and intellectual which our history shows, beginning recently to show hopeful signs of mitigation. The language deciphered seemed to be what I imagined would be a future development of English, a century ahead perhaps.[1]

What was the message? Apparently a future, seemingly following a large scale catastrophe, depicting a culture in which it would be astonishing to question the very human need for active participation in matters creative—a truly mature culture in my optimistic view.

In this chapter, in this book, I hope to show that these practices are more than a need, they are crucial for at least some mitigation of our current blindly following the lemmings to the cliff. For the absence of genuine creative practices denies far too much of our humanly being, far too much for our collective, and individual, health: physical, emotional, spiritual.

---

1 Contact the author for a draft.

And I am suggesting that this wider, more rounded individual and communal living can be helped into being, and maintained, by practical applications of authentic music and the arts, working in goodwill with their sheer life giving enjoyment, so that they naturally become manifest in the meaningfulness of life at the same level that attention to our employment and household are now, for the good of our psychic balance, for the good of our souls.

❖   ❖   ❖   ❖   ❖

THE SUBJECT BEFORE US IS the concept of a New Renaissance, as a requirement in our current collapsing culture. That thought immediately prompts remembrance of the great artists, inventors and thinkers of the historic Renaissance such as Alberti, Brunelleschi, Leonardo, or Michelangelo.

The concept of 'renaissance man' has long been familiar in our language: one who transcends, bridges, the compartmentalisations of the world. Making use of that old phrase, in this essay we are implying that a desirable new world may be envisioned, in which the current habituated all-too-often misunderstandings and rival status claims, even active warfare, between boundaried domains are put down. We wish to erode these now traditional attitudes in favour of co-operative cross-fertilisation and mutual respect and support. Taking this to be the aim, we will take as focus of exposition in this endeavour music and the visual arts.[2]

My vision of the New Renaissance world has the practices of music and other arts well integrated into the cultural fabric. Integrated, and, importantly, centrally meaningful as a prime non-verbal value to all aspects of life—and we must include literature, particularly that liminal art, poetry. These values should be also the practical and non-linear, with expressions tending to the holistic, inclusive as opposed to the narrowly focussed, affirmative of values other than the economic and material.

This is in contradistinction to the marginalisation and commodification of music and arts apparent in our present profoundly unbalanced *soi disant* civilization. Marginalisation (in the UK despite, and arguably because of, Arts Council grant policies) is now so pervasive that in equations of what is officially held to matter in our mainstream culture arts tend simply to be overlooked, despite their (commodified) economic value—seen as meaningless and disposable add-on entertainments: bread and circuses. Art therapies, for example, are often held to be expensive luxuries which NHS Trusts cannot afford, yet they may be less costly in some cases than the lifetime of medication which their success can banish.[3] Nevertheless the

---

2 The initial publication of this essay was as a chapter in *A New Renaissance: Transforming Science, Spirit and Society* - ed. *Lorimer & Robinson 2010*. Lightly edited.
3 Casson 2004 Appendix 4

conventional attitude prevails, while Big Pharm protects its investments.

A more extreme version of this outlook was articulated by experimental psychologist Steven Pinker:

> Cheesecake packs a sensual wallop unlike anything in the natural world because it is a brew of megadoses of agreeable stimuli which we concocted for the express purpose of pressing our pleasure buttons. Pornography is another pleasure technology. ... [T]he arts are a third ... I suspect that music is auditory cheesecake.[4]

Such cultural attitudes percolate down (or through), however much at an individual level one's musical preferences or art classes are treasured. Less tangible values therefore become hard to assert against such prevailing unanchored misperceptions, to say nothing of the here evidenced shadow side of liberalism, where there are no values in the vertical dimension, everything accepted as equal: flatland.

With that in mind we note a pervasive theme elucidated by the far seeing Iain McGilchrist on the somewhat schizophrenic attributes of the left hemisphere outlook:

> Alienation, fragmentation, decontextualisation: the defining features of the modern world were as problematic for art as they were for society ... The predicament of art in the modern period could be said to be how to respond to this challenge.

---

4 Pinker 1997 pp525-32, quoted in McGilchrist 2009 p483, note 43

And its problem is made more intractable by a different sort of deracination—more than just the severance from place ... but the inevitable consequent severance from the roots of all meaning in shared values and experiences, the vast implicit realm from which imagination draws its power'.[5]

Anne Wilson Schaef provided a telling parallel, describing our mainstream worldview as addictive:

Like any addiction, *this worldview absorbs positive attributes like love and then presents them as if they were its own, feeding off nonaddictive energy and, at the same time, seeking to overpower and destroy it*[6] (emphases in the original)

And there is a further slant to this, seen through the lens of art:

One can surely agree with Virilio that the unanchored re-presentation of reality as art, however dislocated or disturbing —an extension of the aesthetic creed, art for art's sake—which is endemic in modernism, is part of a much more profound failure of compassion and an erosion of pity.[7]

The failure of compassion and associated loss of pity can be discerned in almost any news report, and in ordinary encounters in public simply lacking what used to be called common politeness.

---

5   McGilchrist 2009 p409

6   Wilson Schaef 1992 pp96-7

7   McGilchrist 2009 p411, discussing Virilio 2003

But the art and music worlds are not entirely sterile, devoid of empathy and feeling. Heidegger commented on great art that "the artist remains inconsequential as compared with the work, almost like a passageway that destroys itself in the creative process for the work to emerge." And Merleau-Ponty similarly considered that an authentic work of art (and this also applies to music) was not about the work as invention, nor about the artist, but enabled the world to be envisioned (reheard) anew.

There are always some for whom their creative work has nothing to do with ego flattery and everything to do with passionate endeavour to convey deeply held and felt convictions about the world, probably better not verbally articulated, whose works are compellingly 'seen through' to the lived world itself. Anyone who has visited Sandham Memorial Chapel in Hampshire without being profoundly moved by Stanley Spencer's visionary murals of his WWI experiences was surely sleepwalking. In a different though related vein, the contemporary English composer Jonathan Harvey transcended the modernist style he worked in, and is regarded by some as having produced deeply spiritual music.[8] In both cases the experience is drawn through perception of the message, not the messenger.

Such life enhancing values are precisely what my vision of

---

8   His book *In Quest of Spirit* is discussed in chapter 8 of Bk 1

our coming world finds to be *its* mainstream: a world where distancing by conceptualisation, mostly verbal, is complemented or paralleled by holistic direct sensual interaction with what is encountered—Maslow's 'peak experiences' as not exceptional, but commonplace.

As exceptional experiences we feel impelled to make special note of them. David Abram, now carrying forward the phenomenalist enterprise, writes extensively on this topic, and has several tales to tell. Here he is in the Himalayas:

> Across the dry valley, two lammergeier condors floated between gleaming, snow-covered peaks ... I took a silver coin out of my pocket and aimlessly began ... rolling the coin over the knuckles of my right hand. [In] the dazzling sunlight I noticed that one of the two condors in the distance had ... swung out from its path and began soaring back [towards me] ... As the great size of the bird grew apparent, I felt my skin begin to crawl and come alive, ... and a humming grew loud in my ears. The coin continued rolling along my fingers. The creature loomed ... until, suddenly, it was there—an immense silhouette hovering just above my head, huge wing feathers rustling ever so slightly. [T]he coin dropped out of my hand. And then I felt myself stripped naked by an alien gaze infinitely more lucid and precise than my own. I do not know for how long I was transfixed, only that I felt the air streaming past naked knees and heard the wind whispering in my feathers long after the Visitor had departed.[9]

9 Abram 1996 pp23-4

This description of oneness precisely illuminates the connections with art and music I am trying to put across. Despite its prose form, there is I think a poetic sensibility at work in the quoted passage which gives me and hopefully you that 'seeing through' to the lived world mentioned above. Much despised tree huggers can know this feeling, as can musical improvising groups focussed wider than the notes and away from egoic virtuosity. Practitioners of Goethean science should also recognize it.

There are, as may be expected, many art and music creators with similar intentions, unconscious or not, as Spencer and Harvey, but with less skill, talent, or luck of circumstance, who do not gain attention from mainstream culture arbiters, but nonetheless attract devoted intelligent local appreciators of their work. This contrasts with the legion of lesser talents currently enjoying high profile media favour because they are assiduously following the cultural fashions, often entirely consciously, and even cynically. I am here taking it as a given that art and music creation focussed entirely consciously—too easily becoming self-consciously egoic——almost necessarily excludes that "vast implicit realm from which imagination draws its power" to re-use McGilchrist's telling phrase.

The works of these latter are life denying, because self-regarding, and produce only the shiny surface to focus on, no depth to 'see through' to the lived world: mirrors which reflect nothing except the smirk of the inventor. Too many in our sick culture have lost the perception to spot the inauthenticity of such work, or the courage to challenge the 'experts'. My wished for future redeems that loss, via the regaining of mutuality, mutual trusting, through the lenses of authentic music and art, authentically perceived, seen through. And this is spiral, for a revelatory experience opens us up to expectation, which affects what we can (and will) create; and via inter- and transpersonal connections, what others will create, and so round, all of which widens our perceptions of 'the other' as a feeling being like us, open to trust. True art *is* life, non-verbal metaphor as it were, and co-creates with us the better, more authentically felt parts of our life. It is life enhancing.[10]

❖ ❖ ❖ ❖ ❖

THIS VISION OF VERBAL, LINEAR THINKING demoted to be equal to a promoted non-linear is not at all new, appearing here and there in many forms, places and times, which there is not space here to explore. However, a series of published documents on the state of the world can be seen to exhibit a tenuous trajectory through time in the admission into their reports of considerations other than the material. Indeed their changing definitions of possible content show, I submit, and this is why I choose them for illustration, something of the recent history of new

---

10   This is added to in Music Book 1, appearing in several places.

thinking and concern for the state of our culture.

The MIT 1972 report for the Club of Rome's Project on the Predicament of Mankind firmly adheres to discussion of material resources and socio-political trends, though the absence of consideration of value systems was noted by commentators on the draft, answered by "The present model considers man only in his material system because valid social elements simply could not be devised".[11] The term 'devised' here suggests eloquently a focus on measurement as sole validity. Similarly in a UK government discussion paper on Future World Trends the potential, even practical, values of non-material factors are simply not considered.[12]

Two years later UNESCO published a report of a Round Table on 'What kind of world are we leaving our children?' This topic left room in its formulation for consideration of music and arts values, which were taken up by a couple of contributors. Philip Noel-Baker, recalling perhaps Rousseau's *Emile or On Education*, called for "investment to combat the darkness of the mind ... I would found our education on music", citing Kodaly, Suzuki, and a now largely forgotten English educator, Charles Fry, who founded his academy for merchant navy officers on music and gymnastics, among whose old boys during WWII were no less than seven Royal Navy admirals—

11 Meadows 1974 p188
12 Cabinet Office 1976

comment not needed![13] Elsewhere in the report Aurelio Peccei asserted that

> the concept of responsibility *and beauty* must take precedence over the concepts of needs and rights ... [the] responsibility regarding what we are doing and planning".[14] (emphasis added)

The importance of beauty cited here arrests because of the rarity of such an assertion in our materially oriented world. The personal disciplines required for meaningful musical and artistic expression cannot help but inculcate responsibility for self, which then infuses all other actions, an inculcation tragically subverted by the frustrations of living in a depersonalised and over-materially oriented world.

I am talking about authentic music and art here, not the self-serving cynical constructs, surfaces without depth, metaphorical or literal, which gain plaudits in our sick culture for providing The Shock of the New, a concept displacing beauty, falsely equated with creativity. However the unexpected award of the Turner Prize in 2009 to Richard Wright's understated filigree works rooted in fine-art beauty traditions *might* have indicated a welcome change of direction on the part of art grandees and hopefully also other arbiters of culture. Perhaps in the 2020s such signs may reappear . . .

---

13 Noel-Baker 1978 p81
14 Peccei 1978 p121

And then the Club of Budapest report in 1997, written by that fine inclusive mind Irvin Laszlo, in a chapter on resources for revisioning, devotes an entire section to art and religion. The coupling is noteworthy, recalling Joseph Campbell's insight that purposes and actions in the domain of religion were taken over by the arts during the modern period. Laszlo writes:

> In great art and literature, and in the foundations of the spiritual experience, we can experience a deep source of inspiration for living and loving, and harmony with nature. ... Despite [art's] different modes of expression and its own criteria of excellence, it is nourished by the same fundamental source as science: insight into the nature of human experience. ... Great works of art and literature ... attain universality. They socialize us ... giving us insight into the relations that bind us to each other, and to nature. Achieving the true potential of art ... *may be crucial for our future*'.[15]

If the pessimistic conclusion of McGilchrist is indeed right, that the atomising narrowly focussed left hemisphere and its teachers is succeeding in blocking off the more life affirming and holistic attitude of the right hemisphere, as the oscillations through the history of the Western world of left and right brain hemisphere views-of-the-world proceed, then Laszlo's insight in the last phrase quoted above is also correct, and highly important, for the right hemisphere has important roles to play in the mediation of art and music, which can therefore be an aid

---

15   Laszlo 1997 p87. Emphasis added

in warding off that fate of impoverishment and culture wide schizophrenia which in the end cannot but lead to full cultural collapse.[16]

More recently, though, there are further signs that our culture is changing towards a broader understanding. Archaeologists have in recent times begun to consider the acoustics of ancient sites, which might give clues about their original builders usage intentions, thus attending to a non-visual sense. Paul Devereux produced the first survey of this work.[17] He was also on the founding editorial team of a new journal accepting papers exploring ancient consciousness through archaeology.[18] Issue 1 included an interview with landscape archaeologist Peter Fowler, who had taken to imaginatively painting landscapes as a complementary way of approaching his work. A movement away from, or at least complementary to, interpretation of the past purely via material remains is clearly underway, and it would be reasonable to expect it to develop that growing inclusiveness in further ways as yet unspecified: a step maybe, I submit, and hope, towards integration of the arts and work worlds.

The trajectory I have tried to indicate as inhering in those reports could be perceived as intrusions in the mainstream

16 McGilchrist 2009 pp103ff & elsewhere. More widely perceived now in the 2020s

17 Devereux 2001, and see the review extended in this volume: Ch.5. The archaeology of sound in ancient sites.

18 Devereux et.al. 2008 - *Time and Mind*

world of 'authority'—reported though it too often is by the over powerful media as unassailably homogenous—by smaller cultural streams on the other side of the watershed, emerging from underground. Under various names—'New Age', Altern- ative lifestyles, Cultural progressives—these streams are cutting channels in our culture which taken collectively begin to add up to at least the possibility of a better future, a future which seeks to empower local communities as opposed to centralising tendencies by government, privileging inter-personal relations as antidote to sweeping generalizations of 'citizens' as 'work- force' and 'consumers', and pays attention to psychic develop- ment (self improvement stream) and therefore as corollary, arts and music perceived as more than mere entertainment, but integrated into the fabric of life. Laszlo had this to say:

> While there is undoubtedly a lunatic edge to this vast movement that is escapist, introverted and narcissistic, there is also a core that is intensely significant and hopeful ... It indicates the emergence of a different mind-set: the evolution of a new vision.[19]

And in more recent times the signs are that, in parallel with widening perception of the crises facing us, at first focussed through the over hysterical and hubristic lens of climate change, these conservatively dismissed movements are moving closer to mainstream approval. What is also illustrated though is how

---

19 Laszlo 1997 p89

slowly new ideas, mindsets, propagate into the world of power-over, as a consequence of the inevitable clinging to stasis in fear of loss of that power.

❖ ❖ ❖ ❖ ❖

RETURNING TO ART AND MUSIC, examples abound of events and organisations aimed at empowering young persons (our future) by nurturing their creativity. The founder of one, The Power of Hope (since 2008 in Britain as LIFEbeat) which supports disadvantaged peoples, and seeks via music to help young people to find courage to live successfully, commented "We can become creators of the culture we want and not just consumers of the culture we have"[20] Another example is the Khayaal Theatre Company, which tours England with plays and music striving to represent Islam positively, extensively consulting young Muslims in Britain in order to popularly present complex issues, with the mission to draw out faith to enrich art and draw out art to enrich faith, precisely the kind of integration discussed in this essay: nothing new really, but arguably in danger of oblivion at mainstream level, though burgeoning in the so called 'alternative' world.

Both these examples of purposive uses of arts as not mere entertainment are taken from an issue of occasional newspaper (now in magazine format) Positive News, and these pointers to

20 Resurgence magazine ran an article on it: issue 248, May/June 2008, Co-founder Charlie Murphy talks with Rupert Sheldrake.

the world discussed sit with empowering endeavours aimed at adults, such as at the Findhorn Foundation, many other establishments hosting 'alternative' courses and workshops throughout the land, and community building activities such as Participative Spiritual Inquiry work and communal musical improvisations as approached by for examples Rod Paton's Life Music and the Music & Psyche Network.

Such work can have practical applications as well as creating and maintaining strong interpersonal links. The Music & Psyche Network found that an initiatory improvisation prior to business meetings created harmony and respect in the ensuing verbal discussions, not unlike the moments of gathered silence before Quaker business meetings. The Participative Spiritual Inquiry work specifically aims at building communal working structures without hierarchy, though it is not, so far as I know, as yet using any art or music modalities to facilitate its work.[21]

Such creative endeavours are too easily perceived as educationally supplemental, separate from the 'important' acquisition of pre-digested information designed to make its receivers useful to the economic body politic: Schooling instead of education—the power of endemic compartmentalisation. The findings, confirmed in later work, that listening to music positively enhances learning, has made no noticeable dent in mainstream

---

21   Similarities and differences between these two organisations are discussed in Bk.1, Ch.9

education provision: sales of Mozart recordings sky-rocketed for a while, since his music was used in the experiments—to the unnecessary detriment of vast quantities of other fine music.[22]

Much of what is written above points to a possible reintegration of music and the arts into the fullness of life. There is currently a profound rift between the official, mechano-economic body politic and what each individual counts as necessary for a satisfactory life. We all (barring various modes of pathology) spend some time creatively, from a level as simple as keeping pot plants to as complex as may be found among dedicated artists, musicians, architects, engineers, to name but some. We direly need to discard our narrowly divided culture and its excessive bureaucracy: being a musician as I am does not mean I am incapable of (say) creating furniture, looking after a baby, or understanding scientific method. The common prejudice that I am 'only' a musician denies that capability.

These thoughts are not suggesting an intrusion into privacy by unwelcome officialdom, but an expansion of individual ways of living into co-operative governance, replacing an un-feeling and over-weight bureaucracy which acts as if 'citizens' are untrustworthy. Show a person trust and trustworthiness will tend to follow: deny that and the individual will strive for personal autonomy in whatever ways are still open: anarchic, psycho-pathological, or in honesty and spirit towards all others.

22   Rauscher 1993

Two

Some musings on sonic healing modalities[1]

THIS CHAPTER IS ABOUT the healing aspects of what all healthy humanity has: innately assimilated music. We all know what we like, and that defines our natural or at the very least cultural musicality. The thesis proposed here is that organized sound, and therefore music, affects states of consciousness. A more precise description is that resonance with vibratory field properties of the human organism are what underlies our sonic propensities. Choices of tuning will be shown to have effect.

Back in the late 20thC it was possible to fairly easily collect all available books in English on the esoteric aspects of music, including healing properties. And I did ! Many of those volumes focussed on aspects of human consciousness as source as well as receptacle of musical sound: books by writers, investigators and practitioners Sri Chinmoy, Joscelyn Godwin, Hans Cousto, Kay Gardner, and others. These books occupied a modest length of bookshelf at that time. Now there are many more publications, and many more people involved in the area, as can be discerned on the *Sound Travels* website,[2] which lists more than a hundred new and old teachers and practitioners.

---

1   This chapter is a writeup of notes for a presentation to a conference of the *Quaker Fellowship for Afterlife Studies* and *The Friends Fellowship for Healing*.

The Appendix paper *Tuning, Resonance and Consciousness* is a fuller discussion of the concepts and of the methodologies claiming them outlined in this essay, including a careful look at the various, and conflicting, ways which have been adopted to explain consciousness in the absence of direct physical perceptions, through microscopes or other instrumentation. (What ! Nothing there?)

❖   ❖   ❖   ❖   ❖

WHAT IS SOUND?

'SOUND' IS MULTIPLY DEFINED in our English language: we are dealing with a whole collection of related life aspects. Here are some definitions:

1. Sound: A strait connecting two bodies of water, with the connotations of swimming, water, sea. Water has long been recognised as symbolic of the emotions, which means that music, as an untranslatable 'message', necessarily connects with emotions, which are also untranslatable. And water is the most powerful of the elements. It takes its time, but will eventually cut through rock: think for example of the Grand Canyon in the USA.

2. Sounding: Swinging the lead from a boat to establish the depth of the water. Necessary prior to modern technology.

3. Sound: The result of vibrations in the air or other medium, a standard scientific definition.

4. Sound: Metaphor applied to an individual person, object, body or organization perceived to be in good condition, free from defect, fit for purpose. Healing intentions certainly imply this.

Related words are 'tuning' and 'resonance', meaning finding the right pitch for the task in hand, bringing into harmony, and being in sympathetic vibration with: much used metaphorically. 'Entrainment' is synonymous, as is 'coherence'. The latter term is favoured by science.

Readers will know that 'tuning' with respect to musical instruments adjusts pitches to the desired levels; 'resonance' refers to environmental reactions, echo effects and the like; and 'consciousness' is what we need in order to perceive and understand the ambient sounds and structures thereof within our milieux.

An example of resonance is observable in a group of same swing time pendulum clocks, such as all constructed to one second beats, beginning with their swings randomly out of synchronicity with each other. They will then gradually and inevitably move towards beating together, synchronously. On another example level, women menstruating proximally have been noted to entrain their individual processes.

The world and our existence in it is highly complex, particularly, as my line of perceptions asserts, in the so called non-physical realms. We can *know* matters, occurrences, the thinking mind does not, or not immediately; we can become aware of persons near to or important to us, both in and out of physical proximity. Our human resonations with our environment and each other, which are easily (and often) masked by egoistic concerns, reminds us that we have physical, electromagnetic and spiritual bodies. The latter are the source of the urge which, among other profound connectivities, impels that dear one to non-physically contact us when she or he dies, or suffers an accident, needing us to know.

❖ ❖ ❖ ❖ ❖

THE BODY VIBRATORY

ALL THE ABOVE ARE INDICATIONS of our fundamentally vibratory bodies, with which we interact with all the various vibrations in the world and cosmos around us, including the sounds which we interpret and create formally (composing), less formally (conversing, improvising), or spontaneously (happy shouting, or vocally reacting to an injury) etc. Other vibrations in our bodies noted above include not only the electromagnetic, which gives us inter-connectivities opaque to our limited senses, but also the physically rhythmic such as heartbeats and breathing, which generate sound, not usually auditory to the natural state of our hearing, but nonetheless existent.

In addition to these, there are a number of mechanical

movements in the body which are rhythmic, also generating sound. These result from the actions of breathing, heartbeats, and less obviously circulation of the blood, the sounds of digestion, and of the skeletal joints—walking, for example, though other movements may not be rhythmic. These sounds can all be heard with practice, with the aid of stethoscopes, or using earplugs to 'hear' the vibrations internally.

All these sounds and rhythms contribute to the resonances which permeate our livingness, the within and without of our bodies. Many, indeed most, of these resonant relationships occur according to the sonic harmonic series. We may consider that to be a humanly and other lifeforms physical, and cosmic, condition: there lies one of the sources of our music making.

En route to the cosmos, the Schumann Resonances, an electrically charged atmospheric layer between the earth's surface and the Ionosphere, has a standing wave of 7.8 Hz, usually, which matches the brain waves of a peacefully resonating body which is in deep meditation. Sometimes that standing wave varies, reflecting some strong mass emotion from the planet's surface, such as the collective fears evident as our *soi disant* civilization undergoes current increasing demolition. This is *felt*, whether we know it consciously or not.

We humans may be the dominant lifeform on this planet, but we are not its masters, and should carefully note that disastrous misapprehension.

❖   ❖   ❖   ❖   ❖

TYPES OF SOUND

WARFARE. Let us call this negative uses. No doubt through all human history warriors have shouted, an attempt to intimidate the enemy, and to cover their own fear. Oriental martial arts have refined the shout into a precise sharp sonic weapon. Nazi bombs on Spain in the 1930s had whistles attached, so that they screamed as they fell, inculcating greater fear. And in the 1970s technological sonic weapons were researched by the major powers. The infamous Professor Gavreau in France contrived to be absent when his devices were tested, resulting in the deaths of assistants from ruptured spleens and other tragedies.

It appeared to be difficult to provide adequate shields for the operators, and many such researches I believe were abandoned for that reason, at least at that time. Maybe such nefarious practices are more effectively hidden now, or outsourced: a dark surmise.

VOCALISING. Ordinary speech sounds are perhaps the most common sounds we hear within our urbanised culture, except for traffic. They can tell us much about the person speaking. Is the voice monotonous or richly modulated? How we speak our names informs the hearer how we expect to be treated, and tells ourselves too, if we pay it attention. Bashfulness in speaking ones name is tellingly prevalent: so many people do not believe in themselves; or to put it another way, too many people (in our Western world at least) are adult fearful children.

All aspects of spoken soundings are involved in this informative aspect: Pitch changes; nasal modulation or not; body resonance—where does the sound connect with our body: in the head? in the heart area? This is projection. Is the sound veiled or not: Breathing patterns indicate shortness or fullness of breath: fast or slower. All these describe how we sonically and so personally front onto the world. Conscious discernment is much absent, though I am inclined to suspect the occurrence of unconscious perceptions having plentiful effect subliminally.

SINGING. The spoken word is largely mediated from the left brain hemisphere, intellective meaning being dominant in Western culture owing partly to the abstract quality of our alphabet, which may be compared with where pictographic writing is or was utilised, tending to indicate more psychologically balanced cultures. Such are found largely in antiquity —modern full Chinese writing, though, represents a midpoint between the alphabetic and the pictographic, which may be a useful clue to the Chinese collective culture.

Note that when we sing, the words are relocated at least to some degree in the right brain hemisphere, the more holistically nuanced area, along with the music. Here the greater feeling and emotive meanings come to the fore.[3]

TONING. Ancient traditions of this abound all over the globe, non-intellective communion through sound, often produced in harmony with surroundings. Mantras are related: although us in the West are more familiar with mantras from the Orient, Africans have them too, in their own ways, tending, in East Africa where I have heard some, to be verbally more extended than those in the far East, nevertheless rhythmically repeated to gain the intended state of *communitas* (which strictly means community without status structures). Religious retreat communal speakings and chantings also come under this head, much as in traditional Monasteries and Friaries.

SHAMANISM is led to from Toning. Mircea Eliade described shamanism as

> a primitive religion, in which the shaman is also a magician and medicine man; he is believed to cure, like all doctors, and to perform miracles of the fakir type. But beyond this, he is a psychopomp, and he may also be a priest, mystic, and poet.

Strictly, 'shamanism' is a religious cum medicinal phenomenon of Siberia and Central Asia, but in modern times the term has come to be used much more widely for description of equivalently similar contexts throughout the world,

---

3   See Schlain 1998 & McGilchrist 2009

in which the ecstatic experience is considered the religious experience par excellence, [and] the shaman, and he alone, is the great master of ecstasy [4]

And this brings us to the tool pervasively used in that context: Drums. Why drums? Anthropologist Andrew Neher suggested that the widespread sonic frequencies emanating from a drum beat, together with the repetitive rhythms employ-ed, often in the brain rhythm ranges of day-dreaming or meditation, and in relaxed wakefulness, all combine powerfully to charge the whole body with energy.[5] Cataleptic states were likely to ensue consequent on extended time practices. Such ceremonies were used for healing, as well as purely religious purposes—if there is any real distinction here.

All the above notes carry an implication of *meaningfulness*, structures of a wider understanding which touch on and contribute to how we hear and create music, whether purely for pleasure, or for more purposeful reasons, which we now consider.

❖   ❖   ❖   ❖   ❖

HEALING MODALITIES

IN THE PRESENT DAY, REVIVAL of a very ancient art is becoming

---

4   Eliade 1964 p4
5   Neher 1962 pp151-60

pervasively and commonly more widely recognised in the Western world: healing with sound and music, which has links with classical antiquity as well as, probably, ultimate origin in prehistoric shamanism, or even prior to that. Here we should note that by 'healing' is meant more than just curing of illness in the conventional Western medical sense. It means to make whole: here there is an implication beyond the notion of physical health. To make whole is to bring into balance, not only within the individual, but also with others, ones culture, the earth, and the universe at large.

This sort of statement tended to be routinely regarded from more academic/scientistic quarters as an example of 'New age' fuzzy thinking, or in the present difficult times 'not following the science' ! But it has a grounding in physio-psychic reality. Therefore healing is applicable whether or not one is 'ill'. We are all imperfectly balanced.

Healing with the Voice

WAYS OF USING MUSIC AND SOUND for healing purposes vary enormously. Toning or chanting continues to be very popular, singly or in groups, often making use of one or other of the several oriental techniques for rousing or settling the chakras— those regulatory energy centres of the subtle body (the body's electro-magnetic field is perhaps the physical counterpart) about which conventional medicine is too often dubious.

Jonathon Goldman, leading American worker with sound who learned overtone chanting with a Tantric master from Gyuto, used a flexible compromise system which he had found adapts easily to suit varying individual needs. Observing that different sound healers use quite different pitches for the same purpose, with equal effect, he concluded that this is not just a matter of differing body resonances in different people, but that a necessary part of the healing process is intention:

FREQUENCY + INTENTION = HEALING [6]

This is true of, for example, the use of Himalayan singing bowls. The maker has an intention that the bowl when struck shall resonate in a particular part of the body, not necessarily related to size. This is borne out in my own collection, in which a small bowl emitting higher pitches than a large one, resonates not in the head, as I had initially expected, but in the abdomen.

Intention, as Goldman notes, is scientifically unmeasurable, but we may expect that intention on the part of the healer needs to be paralleled by belief on the part of the healee, or there is no healing. And indeed there are many medical anecdotes of recoveries which seem to depend on the patients' belief systems. Dr Larry Dossey has compiled a number of those stories.[7] The power of belief and of the unconscious should never be underestimated.[8] The non-physical much affects the physical.

6 Goldman 1992
7 Dossey 1993
8 And the power of fear to weaken, noted in the fear pandemic, 2020 on.

It is appropriate here to note physicist David Bohm's Theory of Soma Significance, which basically means body intelligence—our bodies *know*, even if our egoic minds don't. This implies the necessity for beliefs on both sides of the healing act. If that harmony is present, a healing is more likely, bearing in mind the necessity of the soul's agreement (meaning divine) as to appropriateness and timing.

Iégor Reznikoff, Emeritus Professor of Art and Music of Antiquity at the University of Paris, felt that the fashion for overtone chanting was overdone, since

> There is no sound without harmonics ... to hear them means to open our ears to the natural sounds, and the effect of this is to open deep consciousness, so of course they play a role in healing. ... So we practice making harmonics, but we do it in a very simple way, without tricks of the tongue or throat. The tricks keep you in the external consciousness.[9]

He decided in the 1970s to give up listening to and making music in tempered tuning, because he wanted to hear and use the sounds of pure intervals. It took nine months of only listening to musics of India, Tibet, or African pygmies. Then he gathered a singing group: -

> it was as though a veil was lifted ... I found that the purer the sound, the more remarkable the effect ... We use sound in a very simple way ... then adding some elementary intervals,

---

9 Reznikoff 1994

like a fifth because it gives the sense of space, and some very simple chants of Antiquity. [We worked with] people with severe mental disability from birth who could only sit around, unable to speak or walk ... A group of five or six of us made soft pure sound waves. [There was] one severely handicapped man of 30 years old who had never spoken. After only ten minutes of our singing he began to say some words, then very clearly he said "Maman".[10]

Reznikoff and his pupils also worked with the dying.

A taught course in St Patrick Hospital, Missoula, Montana, on Music Thanatology, was initiated by nurse Therese Schroeder-Sheker who some years previously spontaneously held a very frightened man dying of emphysema, crassly ignored and left to die by the hospital authorities and their minions, and sang quietly to him until, now peaceful, he died.

Music for the living should be engaging, energising, but music for the dying must be quite different, since the dying person is engaged in detaching and releasing: these the music should aid. She taught practitioners to sing rhythmless music based on Gregorian chants, self accompanied on harp, played without strong rhythms, since even simple rhythms energise.[11]

Music Therapy

NOW WELL ESTABLISHED and professionalized, Music Therapy

10   *Op cit*
11   Schroeder-Sheker 1994

is generally carried out in a one to one situation, improvising not only with the voice but also the piano (generally the therapist) and percussion (maybe more often the client). Typically work is with handicapped persons whom other more conventional therapies have not adequately helped. The power of this method is amply demonstrated by the recording of the sessions with the boy Edward, whose only reactions to other humans was screaming and biting. When after several sessions he begins to speak his own name, never before spoken, it is a moment of pure illumination.[12]

Therapies with Mechanized Sounds

ONE OF THE MOST IMPORTANT healers with sound, and also theorist, was Dr Alfred Tomatis, ear nose and throat specialist, considered to be the 'Einstein of the ear'. He died in 2001, having spent the previous fifty years turning conventional views on the ear upside down.[13] He considered that the ear is the primary sense, fully functioning four and a half months before birth, and that the function of sound then is to literally nourish the foetus, perhaps particularly from the sound of the mothers voice, filtered into the high regions by the amniotic fluid. He found that speech defects are caused by hearing and listening defects: if you cannot hear in a certain range you will not be able to voice it. According to him high frequency sounds

---

12   Nordoff-Robbins Archive
13   More description: see Appendix 2, under *Sound and Music in the Body*.

are the more important energizers, because of the preponderance of cells in the inner ear which respond to high frequencies.

He developed instrumentation, the Electronic Ear, which delivers sound via adapted headphones which simultaneously transmit via bone conduction. Because he believed that psychological blocks are often initiated by problems with listening before birth, he electronically filtered the low frequencies out of the sounds. As well as the voice of the patients mother, if possible, Tomatis used Gregorian chant and Mozart, all filtered as described. Why Mozart? Tomatis perceived something pure in the music, which to him points to an ideal listening by that genius. There are more than 200 Tomatis centres throughout the world: their results are highly impressive.[14]

Music for Relaxation

THERAPISTS WHO WORK WITH THE BODY, such as in Reiki, Cranio-sacral or various other kinds of massage, often wish to have quiet music playing in the background to aid their clients to achieve the appropriate relaxed state. The difficulty with this is that most recorded tracks on collections are much shorter than the therapy session, then there is a pause, then there is likely a contrasting track. There are many compilations supposedly designed for relaxation, but the vast majority of those are put together to a cliché formula either by the well intentioned inept, or by those with primary interest in financial gain,

14   Tomatis 1992; Leeds 1995

consequently thoroughly irritating to authentic musicians as well as to therapists.

We are, though, back with the importance of *intention*. Music for relaxation has certain characteristics, and the group Symbiosis worked hard to achieve them, playing live to check out what worked musically, as well as paying close attention to the stated needs of therapists. Their album *Touching the Clouds*, which took two years to create, was tested at Kingston University, London, where it was found that the heartbeats of listeners reduced, thereby encouraging relaxation. These tests resulted in the use of Symbiosis' music at St Bartholomew's Hospital in London as part of a study utilising relaxation recordings to reduce medication in stress related disorders.

Their music is as one might expect slow, partly improvised, with the minimum of rhythmic impulse and an absence of strongly characterized melodies, for those would need to have a pattern of tension and release which contradicts the requirement to be emotionally neutral and non-intrusive. A tall order to make any music *qua* music at all within those strictures, egoless performance being perhaps literally unheard of in the conventional western musical world.[15] It is not 'great' music, but is not intended to be: their *intention*, however, was clear, their skill and judgment sufficient.

❖   ❖   ❖   ❖   ❖

---

15   Lee 1997

SOME RECENT PRACTICES.

Russell Stone was a successful pop singer for a while in the 1970s with his beloved wife Joanna. Then Joanna died, still young: this was Russell's big soul wound, which lead eventually to his taking up psychotherapy as a profession. The work he did became a healing practice via Nada Yoga, the Yoga of sound. He gained an MA on toning and it's effects on soma and psyche, which manifested as Sound Recovery Therapy (SRT). He is a very loving man, having completely come to terms with Joanna's death, which bears on his healing abilities. We gladly note here the well known concept of *the wounded healer*.[16]

Catching the cry. A decade ago I was an active part of the Music & Psyche network, whose aim was to facilitate improvised music between the extremes of outright therapy and purely physical music making.[17] During our development of this work we found that sometimes a participant would find the group sounds literally overwhelming, indicating some deep inner need erupting. If the sounding group caught the pitch of the cry of pain and toned it, the distressed person would 'clear' more rapidly and completely, preceded by a deeper bodily contact with the *sound itself*, with benefit for recovery and thus clearance of the now conscious and therefore released trauma.

---

16 www.soundrecoverytherapy.co.uk

17 See *Participative Spiritual Inquiry and the Music & Psyche enterprise*, Ch.9 in Bk 1

An Indian woman trained as a psychologist in the UK later told me that that procedure had been done in India "for ever" !

Cymatics, the science of making sound visible, was initiated by Ernst Chladni in the early 19thC, who put powders on a metal plate and violin bowed the edge, producing complex patterns in the powder, demonstrating that sound can create, and modify, forms.

This work was taken up a century and a half later by the Swiss scientist and artist Hans Jenny, who produced an at that time sophisticated machine, the Tonoscope, to project sounds into. The large volume recording his experiments, titled by him Cymatics (in the English translation), shows some remarkable pattern shapes resulting from sounds, some redolent of familiar biological forms, including cell division—the patterns are not static, but show continuous formings. Projected vowel sounds make recognisable reflected patterns: 'Oh' for example, produces a ring shape.[18]

Jenny's work was superseded in the late 20thC by the acoustics scientist John Stuart Reid, following his experiment with the remarkable acoustic environment in the King's Chamber of the Great Pyramid, which produced images, some seemingly organic, but also resembling ancient Egyptian hieroglyphs. Reid also developed a machine, which he called the CymaScope, a commercial instrument, with which "cymatic

18   Jenny 2001. Further on this in Appendix 2, p183/4

discoveries will be made [in medical science, and] in many other fields from astrophysics to zoology."[19]

Fabien Maman, French musician, founded the *Academy of Sound, Colour and Movement* in the 1980s, which developed out of a performing tour in Japan, where the local applauding habits were to only clap at the end of the entire show, not after each piece. Maman noticed that the sounds echoed on meaningfully to listeners at the ends of each piece, not displaced and lost by applause, a finding well worth remembering.

This led him to explore sonic effects. Eventually, with the help of a biologist who was also a nun, he demonstrated how sounds can explode cells, including cancerous. I have seen the slides: it is real. As we might expect, the French medical establishment was far less than appreciative. That biologist nun was answering to higher authorities.

Itzhak Bentov, an engineer and also a pioneer in consciousness studies, wrote a lovely little book in which he showed that the atoms, cells, organs and whole body vibrated in harmonically related ratios, together with a fascinating account of what happens to and with that harmony during meditations.[20]

---

19   'About us' in https://cymascope.com And see www.cymatics.co.uk
20   Bentov1978. And see Appendix: *Tuning resonance and Consciousness.*

Tobias Kaye created hand carved wooden sounding bowls, made from different woods to create different types of plucked sound resonances, strings strung across various sizes. It is all about finding the resonance, as with Himalayan singing bowls. His bowl sounds are quiet, and very relaxing. Healing for yourself: hold it, pluck it, feel the vibrations. After more than seventy years working at this Tobias stood down, after accrediting successor bowl carvers.

Brain Sync, founded by Kelly Howells on brainwave research, supplies recorded materials which enhance brain rhythms, and thereby cognitive functioning. This was at its beginning advanced technology.[21] Quote from their brochure: 'Balances left & right hemispheres (Hemispheric Synchronisation) using so called Window Frequencies which reach your body cells.' Instructions are to use headphones, because sometimes the same message is whispered into the left and right ears slightly out of synchronicity in order to feed each hemisphere separately. Subliminal messaging is used, inducing sleep while the work continues. Indubitably powerful. Is it effective? I found, *inter alia*, my reading of printed texts became faster and clearer after several months experiencing their recordings.

The following anecdote says something which I have not found explainable conventionally: During a Brain Sync session

---

21   There is also the similar newer enterprise, *Hemi Sync*, founded by Robert Monroe.

I half fell asleep as I lay on the floor in my room, and found myself apparently lying in a street: the ambient 'atmosphere' seemed curiously opaque compared to my home outdoor surroundings. Some persons standing nearby were conversing. One noticed me lying on the ground, and approached. The vision ceased as he reached me and looked down, and I was back in my room. What exactly triggered that OBE I do not know: something in the whispered message I suppose.

Linda Long, biochemist, used human and plant protein molecules from DNA sequences, assigning tones to all four *bases* (basic types of DNA). Two CDs resulted, *Music of the Body* and *Music of the Plants*. The music so created is intriguing, even fascinating, and certainly has the 'normal' musical patterning we might expect. Her claim is that the music parallels aspects of bodily formations, and so is healing. Most music which we create requires some derivation from the body in order to present it to others, even that electronically presented.

Midori, a violinist of Chinese origin, did something similar to Linda Long, but utilising other sources of DNA. She worked with her scientist husband. The tunes which resulted Midori harmonised. Astonishingly, some of the DNA derived tunes sound like familiar Chopin, or Schubert: perhaps we should note the Romantic period origins, maybe echoing a need for lost feelingness in contemporary *avant-garde* composition. Could this be explained? Positively, we might surmise that music gets into our cells from the Divine world, and the act of composition at its deepest penetrates to cell level, usually unconsciously, retrieving the sounds.

On the Romantic period we may note that the heart is our real human centre, contra prevailing intellectual cognition. Negatively we might suppose an unconscious influence. And Midori being of Chinese origin may have had an unremarked bias. Unfortunately I lost the recording I had of this, probably in a house move.

Sharry Edwards grew up dirt poor on an American farm, minus modern electronic pollutions, living simply on wholefoods without commercial additives. These factors might well have enhanced her hearing compared with us 'civilised' citizens. At the age of five she very nearly drowned, resulting in a modification of her auditory physiology which gave her hearing equivalent to dolphins, who can hear sounds up to c180,000 Herz, compared to the normal human range of up to c.20,000 Herz. Not only that, but she can also 'hear' thoughts, moods, illnesses, colours, crosses, rocks, ... And she is able to vocalise those sounds, octaved down so that the rest of us can hear them. Often her vocalisations *are* the requisite healing force, reportedly.

So she can be described as a shaman, having extraordinary abilities, her 'wounded healer' moment being the near drowning. And as is usually the case with extraordinary people, she was persecuted for it as a child. As an adult she founded Human BioAcoustics as a healing resource business, and developed the concept of "voiceprint", effectively her 'tool'. Definitely a one-off !

And lastly, An old favourite, *Music for Zen Meditation* which I have loved for a very long time: clarinet, shakuhachi and koto played with soulful intentions, and clearly divined feelings—can be found on the web.

❖   ❖   ❖   ❖   ❖

CLOSING REMARKS

THESE ARE SOME OF MANY corresponding reports, and their hints and declarations meaningfully lead somewhere, for us to find as needed.

The 20 year experiments with muscle testing by the extraordinary psychiatrist David Hawkins, who was struck by a powerful spiritual force, which took him a long time to assimilate, produced a remarkable series of 'levels' of human consciousness, in which Reason is trumped by Love, which is in turn below Joy, and that is below Peace. These are fundamental attitudes to life, or, better, fundamentally an inner beingness, an individual's natural balance point in his or her current incarnation. If we encounter a person who is clearly loving, or naturally joyful, or profoundly peaceful, are we not truly affected? This is of itself a healing.[22]

Rare individuals find divinity within and are able to express it in their fashion to us lesser mortals, often without words. These are the great artists, musicians, poets, as well as authentic spiritual leaders. Musicians who play out of a deep love (far from all of them!) like Pablo Casals, move us profoundly with their playing.

This too is a healing.

---

22 Hawkins 1995(2012), 2001, 2003

Three

Flows in the Psyche

A psychological model, with notes on musical thinking and doing, and Symbolisms of spiral and figure of eight forms

> How sour sweet music is
> When time is broke, and no proportion kept!
> So is it in the music of men's lives
> King Richard II, III, v. 42

INTRODUCTION

THIS CHAPTER OUTLINES a psychological description of the psyche in a post-Jungian model. Some chapters in the historical essays which follow make structural use of this model. Music, as much loved and near universal pervasive aspects of humanly being, naturally therefore also infers ordinary day-to-day hum-an activities. The model provides succinct perception of meanings, helping wider understandings of the sentient uni-verse in which we live.

Anthony Storr, respected psychologist and writer, tackled the issues of the relationships of music to the human being by arguing "that music originates from the human brain rather than from the external world",[1] which statement is a mite bereft of outer origins actually having a part to play, not to mention the influence of feeling, the heart, which ancient Chinese tradition regards as central to humanly being, not the brain. Discussing sonata form, Storr asserts:

---

[1] Storr 1992: 51.

> The pattern of contrast, conflict and final resolution so
> characteristic of sonata form applies not only to relations
> between the sexes but to many other dualities [as for example]
> critics appraising novels as sonatas in words ... conventional
> forms in both arts are based on archetypal patterns ...
> Symmetry is one such pattern: stories are another.[2]

An archetype in this Jungian context is an innate universal psychic pattern which is skeletal until filled out uniquely by each human individual as their life experiences connect with it. At root it is related to instinct, that force which observation shows that in lesser evolved creatures generates fixed patterns of behaviour more or less identical in each individual, such as birds returning across continents when needing to construct nests, or fish returning similarly to their birth places in the headwaters of a specific river.

We may postulate another connection between music and the psyche, which may also imply encoded archetypal patterns, perhaps not confined to the brain alone, and not so simple. In this case there are distinct dynamic movements involved, specifically the several species of psychic change which derive from our reactions to life's ongoing challenges in the context of our individual natures, informing our responses from minute to minute and also through the larger span of a lifetime, as we hopefully become increasingly mature and as a consequence

---

[2] op.cit.: 83

change bodily as well as in our outlooks, and so develop increasing modes and methods of coping with challenges—coping with life !

In the sense that some essence of an individual appears to persist through the vicissitudes of life, or to persist in re-appearing after changes, Storr's notion does have validity.

However, human personality is formed gradually, the complete individual 'theme' only manifesting after considerable inner growth, to say nothing about physiological changes—can the adult always be discerned in the child, or the ancient in the young hero?

Furthermore, some changes are archetypal in that all who survive are faced with them, responding individually to the challenges they represent, successfully negotiating them or not. One such change is the transition from child to adult, another is the 'change of life' particularly but not wholly associated with women.

What particular musical forms necessarily and only represent these changes? Lewis Rowell associated a simplified perception of such changes with variation form:

> I venture to suggest that the popularity of variation in world music is due to its psychic symbolism: the preservation, development, and reinstatement of identity of the Self during the passage through life[3].

---

[3] Rowell 1983: 179

The considerations mentioned above seem to suggest something different, possibly more complex, than basic variation form, though related. Some clarity may emerge from examination of the psychological model of Californian analytical psychologist Gareth S. Hill.[4] Apparently I was the first to perceive applications to artistic creativity.[5]

❖ ❖ ❖ ❖ ❖

THE PSYCHOLOGICAL MODEL OF GARETH HILL

HERE WE NEED TO PROVIDE A HOPEFULLY not too abstruse description of the model: the necessity becomes clear as the reader may perceive in some of the history chapters that a particular clarity has been achieved by the overlay of the model on the subject, not otherwise expressed. I do hope this ploy is successful.

The model was developed from thirty years of observations, directly of Hill's clients and indirectly of many others through his supervision work. The concepts utilized are founded on C.G. Jung's identification of contrasexual properties in the psyche, which he named *anima* in men, and *animus* in women. These concepts have been all too easily distorted by the prevailing patriarchal worldview, principally by a tendency

to equate anima, women, feminine, soul, feeling, Eros, and the unconscious; and to equate animus, men, masculine, thinking,

---

[4] Hill 1992.
[5] Personal communication

> Logos, and consciousness. ...

> Jung defined *animus* and *anima* as archetypes, placing them fundamentally outside any single historical or cultural manifestations ... But we are blinded to the implications of this fact as long as we are ... confusing the archetypal patterns of masculine and feminine with the corresponding social role characteristics of masculinity and femininity. Jung appears to be as guilty of this blind spot as anyone[6]

But we in the West are now in a culture in which gender roles are less narrowly defined and separated than in the cultural milieu that Jung occupied, a context which has allowed, probably encouraged, Hill to move beyond the patriarchal confusion, which he does terminologically by reserving to gender the terms 'male' and 'female', and the terms 'feminine' and 'masculine' to qualities which can appear in either gender.

Teleologically his model seeks to resolve the difficulties, first by the

> conceptualisation that animus and anima are the archetypal ground for the experience of *otherness* ... only knowable in our imagination, essentially a mystery; hence it finds its elemental expression in the image of the opposite sex for most of us.[7]

Secondly his model takes account of theoretical work done by successors to Jung, in particular James Hillman's suggestion

---

[6] *op. cit.* p177/8

[7] *op. cit.*

that both sexes have both anima and animus; and the identification of the elementary and transformative aspects of the feminine principle by Erich Neumann, for which, following other writers, Hill substitutes the terms *static* and *dynamic*, to facilitate equivalently nuanced application to the feminine and the masculine.

Two concepts developed by Heinz Kohut are also assimilated into the model: *mirroring*, implying that we see in others aspects of ourselves, for example that which we dislike in others mirrors aspects of ourselves we would rather not acknowledge; and *idealizing*, in the sense for example that the anima image of the other in most males is firstly an idealized formation of his earliest experience of that other—usually his mother, and maybe a sister too.

Hill's model is "a dynamical system, that is, a non-linear system whose qualities follow an orderly pattern within which there is infinite variability or apparent chaos" in the sense of the Chaos theory premise that small variations in input can give rise to large differences in output. Chaos theory aspects will be noted after exposition of the model itself.

> The fundamental premise ... is that four basic patterns underlie all human activity. These patterns are revealed in behavior, motivation, dreams, fantasies, and other aspects of psychic functioning. They operate in family and social systems, and they underlie basic culture patterns.[8]

---

[8] *op. cit.* p3

Psychic processes flow between these patterns within the individual, intersubjectively, and within groups of individuals, such as families, tribes, and nations. The patterns express as two pairs of opposites, the Static Feminine/Dynamic Masculine (SF/DM), and Dynamic Feminine/ Static Masculine (DF/SM). Note: These abbreviations will be used extensively within following chapters.

An individual may occupy any one of these polarities at different stages of development, *importantly* perceiving the opposite pole as *other*. Hill suggests that the principles of feminine and masculine, and the static and dynamic differences between them, "are perhaps the most fundamental patterns in all of life". All four "participate in the apparently equally fundamental attributes of positive and negative". Some account of these opposites and attributes is provided by Figures 1 and 2 (next 2 pages).

Orders. rules,
systems, standards.
Hierarchies. of
meaning, value, truth.
Persona.
The Great Father
STATIC MASCULINE

Goal directed drives.
Initiative.
Individual will.
Linearity. Grandiosity.
Technology.
Dragon Slaying Hero.
DYNAMIC MASCULINE

STATIC FEMININE

Undifferentiated
wholeness.
Uterus, Harmony
with all nature.
Being in the divine
scheme of things.
The Great Mother.

DYNAMIC FEMININE

Disorientation.
Transformation from
the known order.
'Altered states'.
Imagination, play,
creativity.
Dionysos, the dancing
Maenad. The Trickster.

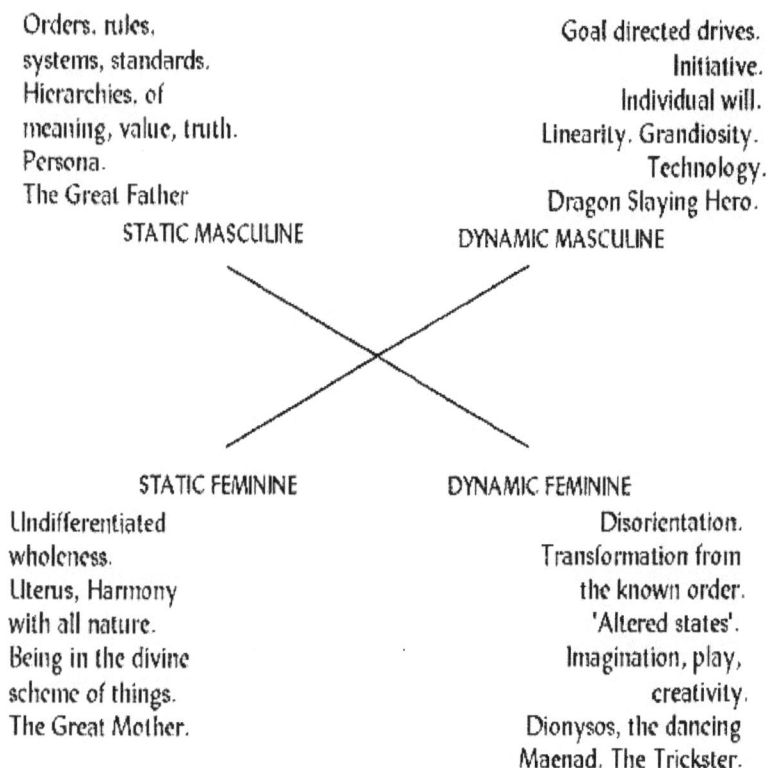

Fig. 3.1 Positive feminine and masculine polarities. After Hill

Rigidity in ordering.
Complacency.
Self righteousness.
Inauthenticity.
Pettiness.
The Saturnine Senex

Inflation.
Willfulness.
Rape, directed violence.
Life taking technologies.
Disregard for environment.
The Despot.

STATIC MASCULINE   DYNAMIC MASCULINE

STATIC FEMININE   DYNAMIC FEMININE

Smothering entanglement.
Inertia.
Stuporousness, mere
existence.
The Devouring Mother

Chaotic altered states
leading to emptiness,
despair, suicide.
Depression, addictions,
hysteria.
The Madman or
Madwoman.

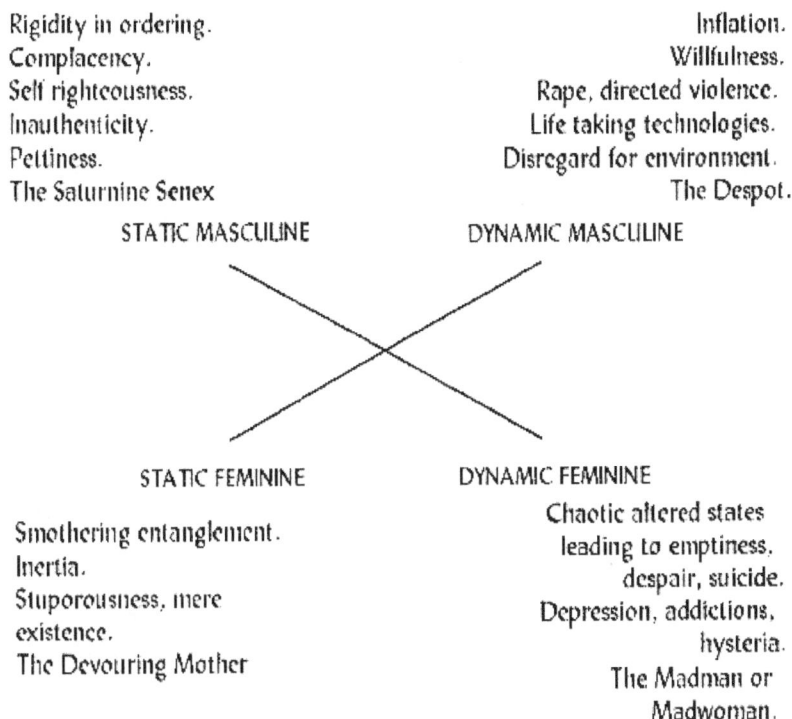

Fig. 3.2 Negative feminine and masculine polarities. After Hill

The full model is developed from these diagrams by expressing the flows from one pair of polarities to the other via two initiatory passages, which Hill's data shows to be ordered, so that there is a normal direction to the movement, psychopathology presenting as a cessation of continuing flow, characteristically oscillation between two poles—getting 'stuck' in life's situations. The initiations are, the Fiery (FI) between the Dynamic and Static Masculine poles, and the Watery (WI) between the Dynamic and the Static Feminine poles. Graphically expressing the idea of flow, the initiations laid onto the crossed polarities diagram changes it to a figure of eight, shown on the next page with the broad essence of its meanings, and the direction of unimpeded flow in the healthy individual.

The "orderly pattern" in the individual psyche Hill delineates in his book by flows descriptive of the whole lifetime, and at a micro-level by flows cyclically occurring many times within a lifetime. He also shows how the model may describe varieties of interpersonal relations, and at the widest level cultural properties and relationships.

However, for the purposes of this book, we remain in the primary arena of the personal flows. They move from the SF, bottom left in the diagram (next page) up and across to the DM, then round, right to left, through the Fiery Initiation to the SM (Static Masculine), and on from there down to the right (DF) and so back to the Static Feminine (SF) through the WI (Watery Initiation). And the cycle can repeat as a further phase of experience/development.

Thus the continuing illustrative flow is fundamentally spiral.

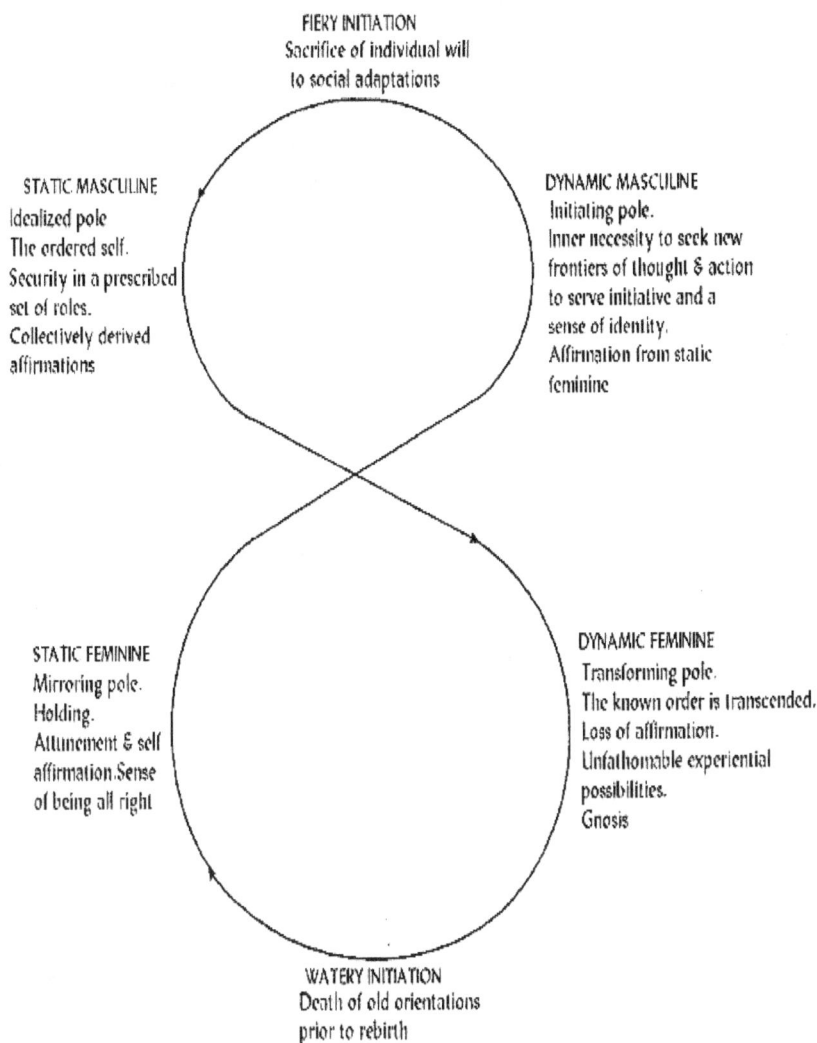

Fig.3.3 Basic flows in the psyche. After Hill.

Viewed as representation of an individual life cycle, a simplified description is presented here. The natural start is at the Static Feminine pole (SF), standing for the nurturing mother or other care person, and therefore the newborn infant too, which soon begins to explore the world, moving away from, but still affirmed by, the mother figure. By puberty, the Dynamic Masculine pole (DM) is the characteristic situation, the young person desiring to get to grips with the world immediately without annoying obstacles, though as yet ill equipped, but eventually the pains of the Fiery Initiation must be suffered before a full role can be adopted within the prevailing culture. Resistance to the Initiation shows in the belief expressed by many young students faced with exams that he/she knows it all, therefore there is no need to sit the exam.

The cultural role position after the Fiery Initiation (FI) is at the Static Masculine pole (SM), typified by the adult seeking to conform to cultural rules in order to gain credit and advantage, positively for example the 'Company man', or the model wife or husband—negatively, the rigid, dominating patriarch.

The Dynamic Feminine (DF) typically manifests as an incursion of insights into the limitations of the individual's world view, which was informed by society's rules. This is commonly known as the midlife crisis, leading to a disoriented period (the Watery Initiation) while the redundant world view disintegrates to allow the new, expanded internal map of the world to be formed. In the life cycle this is typically in old age, a marker which may be changing,[9] in the model a return to the Static Feminine, signifying the new holism.

Experienced positively, the transition from the DF at the level of lifetime leads to a golden late period. Negatively there might be depression, drug abuse, even suicide. If not the latter, then in all likelihood old age becomes a kind of stupor, mere existence. This progression, in the positive, may also be seen as central to what Carl Jung meant by Individuation.

It is important to realize that as a life cycle description this is itself a static masculine construction, teleologically linear. Hill addresses a challenge to his readers:

> The model I describe in this book requires both linear and non-linear thinking. That is, while the model is linearly conceptual and hierarchical, it is also fluid and dynamic, taking an image such as the T'ai Chi. In order for it to be understood in depth, the reader must suffer the tension of these opposites, a sense of ambiguity and paradox.[10]

This is difficult for Western trained thinking, for we tend in such endeavours to collapse into reductive thought. A symptom of that in the reading of his book is the erroneous perception that in necessarily freezing stereotypes for the purposes of

---

[9] Increasing signs of faster developmental growth: a counter to the dire growth of worldwide totalitarian governances.
[10] *op. cit.* p xvi

description Hill is developing a typology reductively containing complex psychic phenomena.

No, he emphasises that his model is not a typology, but a fluid matrix in which "I expect that you will find yourself and others in it with certainty in one moment, only to lose your way in the next". The reader of the book is invited to persist through the sense of confusion in order to seek the deeper understandings that are expected to come through holding the tension of the opposites, which brings to mind Jung's remark that "in any psychological discussion we are not saying anything *about* the psyche ... the psyche is always speaking about *itself*"[11]—meaningful examination of the psyche cannot be wholly objective, the psyche is at once its own 'subject' and 'object'.

An example of the fluidity aspect of the model is the situation of girl children in traditional upper class English life: effectively such young ladies, forbidden to recognise, let alone act out, their masculine attributes, often found a substitute in horse riding, that large strong animal standing in for the forbidden masculine. In checking progress through the model, this would mean missing out the 'masculine' stages, effectively 'jumping' from static to dynamic feminine, thus much enlarging the probability of negative positions—psychic disorder, madness, suicide.

---

[11] Jung CW 9i: para.483

It is interesting to note that the descriptive progression delineating the model which I followed here may be said to represent Hill's professional work with clients. Speculatively, the model would seem to have been built starting with the crossed pairs of polarities, derived from observations of the 'stuck' oscillations of psychopathology between two positions, and completed with the concept of full and free healthy psychic functioning in the flow round the figure of eight, the two initiations having perhaps emerged as the solution to, and the consequence of, the successful outcomes of work with clients.

Finally, the tendency which is available to us to notice introspectively, should we wish to, that in our psychic life we experience movement from order to disorder to order, and so on, and to experience the disorder as chaotic, links to the relatively new scientific tool known as Chaos theory. Hill comments on this relationship with his model:

> Chaos theory tells us that what has been apparent chaos in nature is not chaos at all; rather it is complexity, infinite complexity, which appears chaotic because it defies understanding in terms of the linear conceptualisations that have dominated scientific inquiry for hundreds of years. Our experience of chaos in the psyche can also be conceptualised as a function of over-reliance on the static masculine consciousness ... Feminine consciousness has no difficulty in grasping the underlying order in apparent chaos. It is a thrilling and astonishing development that scientists are

admitting global, holistic thinking to the realm of respectable scientific inquiry.

It is also gratifying to realize that, in analytical psychology, C.G. Jung anticipated these scientific findings. Chaos theory challenges the oft-heard criticism of Jung as being mystical and metaphysical and not scientific, and offers a scientific paradigm, relevant to physical and biological systems, that appears to be completely compatible with his view of the psyche as an open, dynamical system, whose complexity can be elucidated in the rich mythological, alchemical, and religious metaphors he employed.[12]

✦ ✦ ✦ ✦ ✦

MUSICAL FORM DERIVED

WHAT MAY BE SAID OF the overall form arising from the suggested marriage of music and psychological model, now that the nature of the model has been described?

A simple view of the matter might well conclude that, to follow the form of the model closely, there are four moods (let us call them) in two pairs, together with two transitions which link the pairs. Then we might recall that there are actually eight, not four, because of the negative as well as positive versions. This could be treated as simple variation form, with choices as to how the sequences in the model may be preserved —positive and negative at each pole in order, or a positive

---

[12] Hill 1992.: 210-11

circuit and also a negative one. And that leaves out the init-iations, from which it follows that there would appear to be many possible ways in which the model may be utilized as a template for composition.

Taking the music through more than one circuit of the figure of eight may be a way of reinforcing the 'message', so to speak. This would allow some variation treatment to the repeated sections, perhaps indicating a movement of growth, or enhancement, as suggested by Rowell in the Introduction here.

A more nuanced approach, appropriate to the real musical compositional process as it occurs within a composer's work, may be to select some out of the total of eight possible moods; making judgements as to the emphases and therefore extents of chosen sections as reflecting the composers intentions, and maybe extending into a second circuit, thus repeating some poles, but not all: depends where the imagined piece finishes, and how that relates to the starting pole, which for musical form is not necessarily at the Static Feminine. This we might label spiral form, acknowledging the sense of growth, but perhaps all this indicates is some species of complex variation form, with a second order of variations appearing within the second circuit.

All of this could apply to various compositional end-eavours. In purely musical forms utilising Hill's model suggests a complex development of classical sonata form, which perhaps for example Tchaikovsky was moving towards. More obviously pertaining to the model would be song cycle, perhaps aiming at a delineation of human life, or indeed of a life fragment, or more widely of the movements and concerns of whole cultures—how philosophically does the composer wish to work? In fact, that was precisely the form I adopted for my fifty minute song cycle[13]

It is possible to provisionally intuit the use of Hill's model for other artwork types involving dynamic movement: Dance or drama come to mind, as well as novels. How a painter might make use of it seems not impossible, despite the perceived static nature of such work—a sequence of depictions, perhaps. However, all these other than musical possibilities I leave to others to consider in detail.

Attempting further precision in verbal definition is to enter the realms of controversy, not only because of the ambiguity of words but also because here words are second order description of the first order musical or other work, subject then to a second level of disparate interpretation. The final analysis must always be the artwork speaking for itself.

And indeed we can find it so in the descriptive analysis of *The Magic Flute*, in this volume.

❖ ❖ ❖ ❖ ❖

---

[13] *The Night Sea: Aspects of an ordinary life.* See Score samples in Bk.1

SYMBOLISMS OF THE SPIRAL AND FIGURE OF EIGHT

HILL DOES NOT STATE WHY his formulation of the two pairs of opposites shows them crossed, thus leading to the figure of eight when the flows through the initiations are added. There is no doubt a conscious reason, but I allow myself to wonder whether a parallel, possibly unconscious motivation might have been linked to symbolical factors such as offered here.

The figure of eight as essentially a representation of two orbs, one on top of the other, relates to other symbolic representations of the two worlds, upper and lower, occurring in traditions throughout the world, such as the Tree of Life of the Kabbalah, the World Tree on which Odin hung in the Norse tradition, and that small metal object from Tibet, the *Dorje,* held with thumb and finger during certain rituals, believed to encourage psychic connection with the divine world.

The trunk of The Tree is the link between the worlds, the crown in the heavens, the roots in this world, as is the crossover in the usual way of writing the figure of eight in English cultures—8. The associations here ramify on into, as only one example, the symbolism of the cave as this world, with its notional 'Solstitial Gates' opening onto the divine world in the Heavens for sufficiently developed beings, and to admit back to this world souls requiring further spiritual development.

In the Heavens of course is the Zodiac, as another ordering principle—cascades of further symbolisms here. And laid on its side the figure of eight becomes the conventional sign for infinity, the choice of which by mathematicians I suspect dates back at least to the times when the Quadrivium of the Seven Liberal Arts were the prevailing scientific paradigm, at once practical and also symbolic.

The spiral is a symbol of great antiquity, appearing among the 10 to 30 thousand years old palæolithic cave paintings in Southern France and Spain; notably also in the passage of the important, and spectacular, New Grange so called passage grave in the Boyne Valley north of Dublin; inscribed on Celtic monuments, where it is held to signify water (symbolically the Water of Life, or of Death, the unconscious); and elsewhere throughout the world. Spirals spontaneously arise at certain stages of meditation, and also to some people when succumbing to anæsthetic. From the natural world we might also mention spiral galaxies, the vortex of a hurricane, the cochlea in the inner ear, and the spiral form of the DNA molecule, part of the defining centre of life.

Connection with the cycles of life and death is strong and pervasive, spirals appearing in similar myths from, for example, Vanuatu and Ancient Greece—that of Æneus, for one. Spirals have also been seen as protective patterns, placed at thresholds, and are obviously linked to labyrinths, which share with the spiral and the circle the fundamental symbolism of the Border of the Cosmos, and so of its representation, as sacred and also domestic space, and the cosmos of the human heart.[14]

However, any direct mapping of these ideas onto Hill's model would be to risk approaching the patriarchal error discussed in the text above. Symbolic thinking, like thinking about the psyche, requires a similar holding of the tensions of ambiguity, and avoidance of only linear cognition. This parallel is not surprising when one considers the metaphoric language developed by Jung in discussing the mysteries of the psyche.

Enough, enough. Let us pass on.

---

[14] For elaboration of these remarks, consult the essay *Labyrinth: Myth, Meaning & Symbol*. Contact the author for a copy.

HISTORY: SOME VIEWPOINTS

Four

Western Music History: a Jungian perspective

The man that hath no music in himself
Is fit for treasons, stratagems and spoils
The motions of his spirit are dull as night
Let no such man be trusted.

Merchant of Venice v. I. 79

PROLOGUE: WHAT ARE WE TALKING ABOUT?

IT IS A LARGE ENOUGH SUBJECT IN ITSELF, and I don't claim to be primarily either a Jung scholar or a music historian as such. Here we are limited to the history of mainstream European music, conventionally named 'Classical'. Anything more inclusive than that would necessitate a substantial volume of descriptions and analysis.

This was originally a talk presented to the London Jung Club in May 2012, by courtesy of Jung scholar Andrew (now Fred) Burniston, who introduced me at the event. During the presentation various odd problems occurred with the technology of laptop computer and screen projector, which Andrew suggested were indications of 'Wolfgang Pauli' effects: my own psychic influences!

Hmm: comparatively minor effects I think. And another slight possibly oddity slides gently into this chapter, as a small cat apparently appreciating Beethoven: elucidation in the Postscript.

This essay is an expansion of the notes I took to the talk. A short Glossary is added at the end of the chapter.

It will be necessary in the discourse to make sweeping generalisations—some inevitable reductionisms to get across such message as may be appropriate, and possible. Therefore at historical era boundaries we shall take it as read that the boundary is not at a clear place or time, rather that the dying themes overlap the newly burgeoning. So mention of this or that century is convenience for discourse, not implying any precise accuracy. Anything more precise would in any case smack of overly done reductionism. The world is wider and deeper than that. And decidedly more entangled !

After some remarks on extant and older attitudes towards music history I will then give a brief synopsis of the psychological model of flows in the psyche laid out by Gareth S. Hill, which I use as the template on which to lay out the historical developments. The previous essay in this volume gives a fuller exposition.

Why psychological? As analysis and description of human functioning, it would be rather strange if the same functioning could not be discerned in the general and particular activities we invest energy into in our lives. Not least the creative and artistic, notwithstanding Freud's disparagement—defining creativity as impulses denied more direct expression as sexuality or aggression. We may note in passing that many other, supposedly lesser living species, display creativeness. Artistic creativity defines our cultures in ways which, in time, may compensate for our less appealing actions in the world.

❖ ❖ ❖ ❖ ❖

PHILOSOPHIES OF MUSIC HISTORY

Having reached the top of the ladder, one realises it's against the wrong wall.
Joseph Campbell

THE WORLD IS FULL OF VARYING concepts of human evolution, from which the notion of Progress is often pitted against circular arguments about Origins. Here are a couple of old thoughts for illustration of the hubristic notion of Progress:

18thC: Origins are in the noble savage's spontaneous musical outbursts, so music therefore must be the oldest of the arts. This theory pre-dates the modern discovery of neolithic cave paintings, but the assertion might still be true: Prehistorian Steven Mithen proposed that music shared origins with conceptual language via developing nuances in vocal sounds made by early biped groups.[1]

19ThC: Origins are only present subsequent to the times of

---

1 Mithen 2005.

the primitive savage, who had no music whatever, therefore music must be the very youngest of the arts. This is predicated on the truly Victorian inflation that the 'superior modern brain' is needed for symphonies ! As if that is the only sonic activity deserving the sobriquet 'music'. This is a 'truth' to the extent that no large scale 'classical' work has been created within the collective cultural musical activities of traditional cultures. A sense of individualism, of withdrawal from others, is needed for the monumental task of writing to the extent of a symphony: I personally can confirm that. Hence European competitive and individualist culture was and is required for such modernisms.

However, we should note Goethe's warning against too much concern with origins.

The Law of Three comes to mind—an echo of the divine Trinity. Where is the Jungian fourth as completion of the quaternity?[2] Perhaps let that thought sit for now, though a morphology of overly intellectualised 20thC modernism into a freshness which might be compared in some sense with the currently anathematised Romantic period could perhaps provide the feminine fourth. Rudolph Steiner predicted something of the sort, to occur with the English in the current century.[3] We wait to see.

---

2   See the Glossary at the end of this essay for notes on Jungian technical terms.
3   Steiner Followers 1951

Then there are the Great Man theories, proposing that Olympian god-like personalities brought everything into being. Too much, though, of 'modern' art has derived from over-inflated egos, to which the Great Man theory is not merely a supposed correction, but is also too rigidly singular, in my perception. My own observational excursions in East Africa deny it sufficiently perhaps. No musical Great Men there, not in our culture's definitions: everybody joins in, spontaneously, with uplifting emotional effects. No need for any concept of Progress.

And there are theories assuming parallels with the invention of clocks, and with all technology.[4] This one appears to me as narrowly materialist, tending to focus on the craft element and ignore the essential role of the mysterious creative aspect: unconscious content spontaneously emerging from a higher psychological/spiritual level.

I speak here as a practiced composer, aware of unexpected ideas infusing the work from other than the externally oriented ego, which may, and often do, arrive as dream images or sounds, often requiring the early work on a piece, which had been derived initially from egocentric desires, to be fundamentally reworked, or scrapped, as mine often were—on one occasion, several months work had to be: painful, but necessary for the authenticity of the composition !.

---

4   See the Appendix *Mechanisms and Shadows*.

These somewhat conflicting theories may perhaps be seen as partially arising from differential national characteristics—something Jung got into a touch of hot water about on his first visit to the United States, when he mistakenly perceived native American ethnic physiologies in factory workers: his companion said he would doubt there were any *there*, which alerted Jung to the influence of *geographic place* on physiology.[5] As we develop the historical themes we will see something of those differentials manifesting in the music adopted or not by the prevailing zeitgeist.

In my perception music needs to be seen as an expression of the interconnectedness we call culture, or aspects of the origin of that, manifesting through individual efforts deeply or shallowly according to psychological attributes and development. And indeed also according to the nature of that part of the earth's territory occupied, influencing us all too often rather blind humans, by its climates and all its differing living beings: vegetable and animal, as well as varying magnetic currents.

We may, or may not, quite sensibly ask: how individuated is the protagonist? And how separate is the culture, boundaried or not from others nearby or distant and thus perhaps pursuing at least some different paths?

Culture, a word which in this part of the world we who live here unthinkingly mean 'as in Europe', our geographic arena,

---

5   Jung CW10 §§94,948

has had sufficient wealth over centuries to provide enlarged cultural space beyond what is possible where mere existence is crucially dependent on severities of and deficiencies in the supports of climate and physical environment. And we shall also note something of the influence of changing climates as we progress through the history.

Nonetheless musicality always exists regardless of wealth or dire deprivation: it seems innate not only to the human— bird song comes to mind, and other sounds of the wild. Western world wealth provides complex instruments, sumptuous opportunities and spaces (concert halls), and also supports some specialisations: Permanent and passing musical ensembles, conductors, soloists and teachers.

But before delving into history let us take a brief look at the model of the psyche I contextualise the history with.

❖ ❖ ❖ ❖ ❖

THE JUNGIAN MODEL OF GARETH HILL

I FIND THIS MODEL OF PSYCHIC FLOWS a useful and meaningful contextualisation of historical events. The applicability of it to all aspects of life and activity attests to its truth, though it was intended as descriptive of personal and interpersonal growths and developments. Hill commented that I was the first to perceive creative applications.[6] A fuller description is given in *Flows in the Psyche*, previously in this volume. The reader may find the reading here will be benefitted by a consultation there.

Suffice to say, the primary distinction in Hill's model, portrayed in miniature here, is between positive and negative aspects, opposites requiring a resolution, which we may see as Jung's transcendent factor. And there is a direction of flows, from feminine to masculine to feminine and so on, both properties occurring according to the complex movements of life's ongoing experiences. Psychological problems manifest on the model as oscillations between adjacent poles rather than continuing flow.

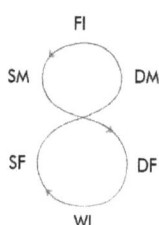

It seems possible to say that in general music is positive ! Of course, all strongly rhythmic music, martial included, charges up the nervous system, sometimes for action, but even Heavy Metal performances do not lead to mass murder or other mayhem (despite Plato's strictures), only localised skirmishes in the press of densely populated Rock events. The song texts themselves are not infrequently quite innocuous.

I believe rather it is the *absence* of music which marks the psychopathic. Despite depictions of horrors, in programme music, on the operatic stage, the effect, I claim, is never equi-

---

6   personal communication

valent to literary depictions. The reason perhaps is that words are closer to the rational, thinking mind, with all its tendency to ego biases, shadow invasions and absence of context. Music comes from, and points to, a deeper place—and can remain beautiful despite depicting negative emotions.

C.G. Jung wrote in a letter to Serge Moreux in 1950: "music represents the movement, development, and transformation of motifs of the collective unconscious".[7] Archetypally mediated music is essentially beyond categories of good/bad, or positive/negative, though presenting through an emotionally mediated face. Hence, on the stage or programmed, the music necessarily takes on a mythical character.

❖ ❖ ❖ ❖ ❖

MAJOR CYCLES

SPENGLER SAW WAGNER AS A culmination, and also the beginning of decadence. Perhaps Spengler was behind the proposal by my Canadian friend and fellow composer John Burke that much of a life cycle could be perceived in the history of western music, from plainsong as the stage of infancy or unconscious wholeness, through 12thC Paris organum as the beginnings of ego consciousness—a technical development to establish position in the outer world, which eventually ran into trouble around the time of Wagner's music dramas, with 20thC

---

7   Jung Letters V.1 p.542

music as the midlife crisis, which he saw as confused and oft-times desperate attempts to locate renewed feminine energy.

Job done? Indeed a telling picture. But no ! not enough. That cycle can be divided into at least two, with sub-cycles developing everywhere, consequent on changing histories, as centres of power and influence shifted within Europe.

1st major cycle: from the Romans to the 14ᵗʰC

I WILL DEAL WITH THIS in a little detail as I suspect that many readers are likely to be more familiar with later periods. I am relating what happened partly to climatic movements which accompanied or presaged noticeable cultural differences until Europe grew wealthy enough to stand up to climates changing: cool periods host relative inactivity, or cultural decline, warm periods support innovations and so cultural growth. Parallels in Hill's model are noted.

The warm climate in the Bronze Age is nicely illustrated in Britain by the Romans growing grapes up by the present border with Scotland.[8] Then the climate cooled towards the end of the Roman period, resulting in the Germanic southward invasion into Italy, which was partly driven by a large volcanic eruption[9] (Dynamic Masculine (DM) moving

---

8   This was also the time when Icelanders colonized the ice free Eastern seaboard of Greenland.

9   Seemingly a partial parallel with the present period of climate cooling

through the Fiery Initiation (FI) and on). This in time duly aided the collapse of the Roman Empire.

Then a largely static period ensued, the mediaeval Little Ice Age, tagged as 'the Dark Ages', when the Church took over from Imperial Rome the role of Great Mother: (the new Static Feminine (SF), Mirroring Pole), and life for many people hardly moved beyond impoverished struggles simply to survive. One may note here Sibelius' comments that there was 'no' Scandinavian music prior to his owing to historically late cultural transcendence of the cold: the last throw of the 17th-19thC Little Ice Age.

Recapitulating, having been brought through the pains of the Fiery Initiation, which can be seen as the official adoption of his wife's Christianity by the Emperor Constantine as a governance unifying move aiming to hold off the upcoming collapse of Empire, we are at the SM Idealized pole again. Plainsong was approved, all other music officially associated with 'debauched' pagans. Plenty of those still around, naturally, aware or not of the official line.

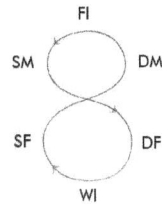

The collapse of Rome we read on the model as the Dynamic Feminine (DF) transforming through the disorienting Watery Initiation (WI) to a new Static Feminine (SF) representing the start of the Dark Ages. As that eased we were lead to the

starting: increasing numbers of volcanos erupting.

Dynamic Masculine (DM, Initiating Pole) representing the subsequent awakening in the medieval warm climate period ushering in the 12[th]C Renaissance, an awakening with commercial expansions which set European invention in motion, aided by the stimulus of imports of objects, persons and, crucially, ideas, brought back from the Crusades, that revelatory culture clash, viewed on the model by the Fiery Initiation (FI).

With Europe waking up, the aristocracy grew interested in more than war and sex, and the Troubadour phenomenon arose: a definite expression of the feminine, and "the last spontaneous outburst of monophony" as well as the "first great flowering of secular art."[10]   We are in the new SM, a positive, following the Crusades.

From 1100 to 1400 France was dominant in European music, largely because it was politically so—Europe's leader.   And musicians began to experiment.   Here we have moved round again through the lower half of the model and back to the Initiating Pole (DM).   Schools began to form, the earliest at the Monastery of St Martial in Limoge, closely followed by the monastery of Santiago da Compostela, from which came the earliest currently known piece in three parts.   Then came the Notre Dame School, featuring Léonin (12[th]C) and then Pérotin (13[th]C) experimenting with parallel melodies.   The necessity for

10   Harman 1962 p94

structure was therefore perceived, consequent on the composing rule of rhythmically independent polyphony.

The Church forbad (Negative SM) more than three parts, and only in triple time, reflecting the divine trinity, the feminine fourth having been dogmatically discarded with the adoption of Christianity by Rome, as we remarked above. Women having status ! Not in that militarized culture ! The feminine element had been meaningfully present in earlier Christian culturally marginal communities: this is important to remember. Note that the spread of Romanesque style architecture at this time can be perceived as also an answer to, or confirmation of, the precious beliefs now wrested by the state—in order to build structurally material yearnings for cohesion. Building forms were very haphazard before that. So we may say some good came out of that process?

In the 13thC polyphonic style, composition rules were quite loose. The old Catholic rules forbidding more than three parts were losing credence. Anything was acceptable provided each voice co-ordinated with the start of each phrase. And so different texts were set in parallel lines. Different texts and different rhythms: a considerable complexity. And the primary interest in this period was to accent the differences in the parts, done with instruments supporting the voices: new wind and string instruments had been brought back from the Crusades.

Now we perceive the 13thC cultural richness: the new

Gothic style cathedrals, with pointed arches copied from the middle east leading the eye up to a (masculine) Heaven replacing the earlier round (Romanesque) arches which lead the eye round again towards the ground—very cathonic, and evocative of the feminine. In parallel came intellectual independence, with Aquinas, and Bacon. And secular, that is, outside the Church, lyric poetry with Dante.

Richness in music—more than a dozen varieties of expression developed out of the previous small handful, which lead to the development of needed notation and the widespread use of instruments together with the application of the keyboard to strings. The keyboard itself can be seen as an expression of European technical inventiveness which was already manifesting.[11] The breaking of the old Catholic Trinity rule was achieved in parallel with this burgeoning of creativeness: the warming climate did its stimulating work.

The 14[th]C saw continued development of complexity in music under the sobriquet 'Ars Nova', requiring increasing sophistication in aficionados and skill in performers, and saw the entry of Italy as a secular musical force to rival the French. Behind the backgrounds of corruption of clergy (selling 'forgiveness' among much else), the Black Death, the 100 years war, the Great Papacy Schism and the Albigensian crusade, the increasing wealth of the aristocracy provided support for am-

---

11 Hindley, 1997.

bitious musicians and composers.

These developments culminated at the end of the century, centred in Avignon (the seat of the French Pope during the Great Schism) and a few other aristocratic establishments in southern France, and became known as the Mannered School. Almost entirely secular in output, the music represented the peak of the medieval ideal: differentiation, with each part rhythmically, melodically and verbally distinct. This represented a full stoppage, no further development conceived as possible: The culture had reached its peak and knew not where to go. We are at the cusp of the Watery Initiation, at sea with no clear direction.

Such rhythmic complexity was not attempted again until the 20thC, following the demise of the diatonic system.

❖   ❖   ❖   ❖   ❖

2nd major cycle and subcycles: 15thC on: differential cultures

WHERE COULD MUSIC GO FROM THERE? In the early 15thC the shadow aspects of the complex medieval ideal emerged in an enantiodromia appearing in the form of the new lyricism (Positive DM round through the Fiery Initiation to the SM) contributed by the Italians in the song, as befitted perhaps their national characteristics.

The English, it is time to note, practiced sonority rather than differentiation, parallel lines harmonically supporting each other rather than contrasting—the smoothness of consorts of viols. This was the first major European influence from England, Dunstable the truly notable early figure: This is expanded on below.

And here we see regional differentiations developing, the unifying dominance of France in diminishment. And then the paths of our model become more complex, no longer defining the peak of the entire continent, but instead diverse leadings emanating from particular regions, partly because increased travels brought ideas, DM energies leading to spreadings to other countries via their own Fiery Initiations: More on this below too.

And from there the diatonic system gradually developed during the 16th and 17th centuries. This was another cooler climate period, following the Mediaeval Warm (uplifting the Renaissance), but by this time mainstream Europe's wealth was sufficient to at least partly transcend such handicaps.

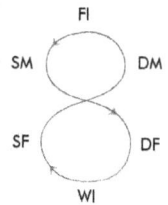

The initial simplicities (SM) were developed (DF down and round up to DM) into the grandeur of the optimistic Baroque, with its high point embodied in J.S. Bach, and after him reborn in the simple elegance of the Rococo style. This was another example of complexity grown too far, transformed through the Watery Initiation and on from there. An enantiodromia again—

always opposites replacing each other. From there, growth, always growth, led to 19ᵗʰC Promethean individualism out-standingly represented by Beethoven, with the approaching new end point showing in (perhaps) negative egoic assertions from Wagner, with Mahler and early Schoenberg delineating the tail end of the dying style.

Then we had the diverse tracks of the 20ᵗʰC, led in various directions by innovating Schoenberg, Stravinsky, Debussy and Bartók. The new philosophical and political dominance of Germany encouraged the widespread adoption of the *intellectual* aspects of Schoenberg's serialism, the more emotionally nuanced French intelligence showing particularly in the work of Debussy. And as a consequence we had the absurdities of High Modernism in 1950s/60s, when so called contemporary classical music lost much of its audience.

I recall at that time, as a personal example, frequently encountering in concert programmes wordy 'explanations' of pieces which took longer to read than the duration of the performance ! Such were the composers' anxiety to be under-stood, unconsciously (presumably) not noticing, or simply not knowing, that explanatory verbosities only project intellectual-ity: music is, or should be, something else. This was definitely the negative SM/DF polarity in a modern circuit !

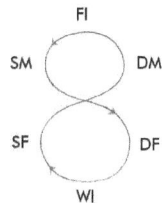

Here are the negative texts assigned to those positions by

Hill, descriptive I believe of High Modernism in the 1950s/60s:

> *Static Masculine*: Rigidity in ordering; Complacency; Self righteous-ness; Inauthenticity; Pettiness, The Saturnine Senex.
>
> *Dynamic Feminine*: Chaotic altered states leading to emptiness, despair, suicide; Depression, addiction, hysteria; The Madman or Madwoman.

❖   ❖   ❖   ❖   ❖

COUNTRIES AND CYCLES

WHEN A THEME HAS REACHED ITS furthest development, as at the end of the 14thC with the Mannered School, or the early 20thC with essentially the ending of any perceivable further development of the diatonic system, the compensatory function emerging from the shadow *tended* to come from a different country, or countries. 15thC Italy, not France, and in the early 20thC parallel dynamic, Bartók, Stravinsky, Debussy—none from Germany.

Viewed another way this can be seen as individual countries having their own cycles of expressiveness and decline, illustrated as circuits on Hill's model, as their historic developments progressed and overlapped with sister cultures. And we should remind ourselves to view the model holistically, not reductively: that a notional position on the model is only relative, the character of the theme very likely simultaneously occupying elsewhere, in a likely opposite, though maybe to a lesser extent.

Apollonian or Dionysian emphases indicate helpfully: thus Romanticism in the 19thC emphasises the Dionysian, so tends to occupy the Static Feminine (SF) to Dynamic Masculine (DM) axis: Great Mother Nature mirroring and affirming Promethean Man. But of course Apollonian aspects were also present, on the other axis—Static Masculine (SM) authoritarianism striving to contain Dynamic Feminine (DF) rebellion structure, with possible chaos in the shadow, appearing as for example loud complaints from the audience at 'wrong' musical procedures by Beethoven, and in the next century near riots in Paris over Stravinsky's innovations.

But then such expressions were followed by 'art' of any sort losing any consensual definitions, growing acceptance of any and all 'novelties', as the modern world attempted to re-find its soul in an overly intellectualised materialistic narrowness. This 'flippant' movement failing, so far, to engage positively with the enantiodromic path, as, we may say, the escape route.

Let us look at England

IN THE MEDIEVAL WARM CLIMATE PERIOD, 9th to 13thC, we English were in good fettle! Not much written music has survived, but that may partly be because we were joyfully 'discanting' improvisationally. We were also ignoring continental preoccupations (sturdy English independence, or island remoteness?—maybe both) and exploring the sonorities of thirds and sixths, as well as fifths. I think the 'discanting' influenced that: four and even five part music is in the Old Hall ms,[12] whereas on the continent, usually only the old Catholic three parters are found.

Following the recovery period after the 12[th]C Black Death, in the 15[th]C we welcomed the first of our Great Musicians, just when he was needed, John Dunstable, who took our thirds and sixths harmonies abroad to France and Italy, infusing the developing forms of the Ars Nova with the sonorities needed for creation of the great 16[th]C multi-part madrigal, chanson, canzone, villanesca. DF and on through the Watery Initiation depicting the transition towards the new musical ideas, culturally needed, at the SF pole.

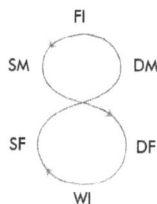

Europe was heading for the Little Ice Age, cool periods through the late 17th to early 19thC, with a last fling right at the end of the 19thC, when the Thames froze over (with recovery through the 20thC, peaking in the 1990s, and turning down circa 2016). But this time, as noted above, compared to the Roman collapse period there was more cultural energy and wealth aiding us through those difficult times.

Nevertheless, prompted by that climatic reason, after Dunstable our sun went down, spawning a relatively fallow

---

12 Largest and most significant collection of early English music.

period illustrated in parallel by the dearth of fine poets between Chaucer and Wyatt (Static Masculine): almost nothing substantially new inventively. Until, after Wyatt came Spencer, who set new literary standards, and, depicting the general cultural meaningfulness of that, we defeated the Spanish Armada, partly by luck !, and so encouraged embarked with confidence on our greatest musical resurgence, with the Elizabethan and Jacobean composers, which included one of the greatest composers of all time, William Byrd, together with Morley, Weelkes, Willbye, Gibbons, Taverner, Tomkins, and also John Dowland, perhaps the greatest singer/songwriter, so far. Forty glorious years. Even localised reiterations of the Black Death failed to deter.[13]

After the Interregnum the restored monarchy brought musical stimulus from France, and another of our Great Musicians came forward: Purcell, the master of English word-setting. After that, as the Little Ice Age grew deeper, English energies mainly went into commerce, manufacture and technology.

The result was that during the best part of two centuries we got used to importing our music (Handel, Haydn, J.C. Bach, and on), for we had insufficient belief in our own, our focus being elsewhere. So that when a resurgence came in the early

---

13 Which occurred in several places, the probable last being in an 18thC Derbyshire village, and during a London excavation for a multi-storey building, in the 20thC

20thC, (the climate warming up again) seeking redemption in folksong roots (Bax, Holst, Vaughan Williams), it was a local affair, threatening to lose out to the habituated influx of continental musical ideas.

And it was in truth a stimulus, as Arnold Bax noted, to native creativity: "it was left to the cranky and contradictory Elgar to prove to the outside world that even the despised Englishman could be a musical genius."[14] Press reporters notably refused to remove their flags from the well worn belief in German superiority—until Elgar's music had sufficiently penetrated their myopic habits and deaf ears.

We may say then, that the DM attempted but failed to sufficiently traverse the Fiery Initiation test, thus not finding a new stability. I consider that right to the end of the 20thC and now into quite other troubles in the 21st, strands of new music have come and gone without gaining solid ground in the culture at large. The future of music is perceivable now in multiple cross-borrowings, catering to a wide variety of tastes. Maybe that is how it should be. Maybe we are beyond the era of the cultural elite lording it over the musics of 'ordinary' folk. Maybe this speaks to the upcoming new Aeon.

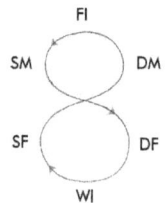

So I leave European history there. Probably our emerging and simultaneously dying global culture is at once too big and

---

14 Bax 1943 p.28

too diverse to entertain anything much beyond half understood banalities for the entire global citizenry.

❖   ❖   ❖   ❖   ❖

REMARKS ON TWO COMPOSERS

HERE I SHALL COMMENT BRIEFLY on aspect of compositional procedures in Sibelius and J.S. Bach which position clearly on Hill's model.

Sibelius often took his orchestral themes through a disintegration followed by a renewed integration, DF through the Watery initiation to SF, which can then develop through to its climax, DM through the Fiery initiation to the SM. In other words, the whole circuit, which we may take as a neat confirmation of Sibelius' structural mastery. This also analogises sonata form as developed by Beethoven, Tchaikovsky and others.

J.S. Bach's music tended very strongly to the Static Masculine (SM) pole, with change boundaries hardly touching the lower half of Hill's model (feminine poles). Decidedly a father figure ! Although, we should note that Jung percipiently remarked on the archetypal circularity of the Art of Fugue.

❖   ❖   ❖   ❖   ❖

THE TRANSCENDENT FUNCTION

Most people use music as a couch; they want to be pillowed on it, ...

But serious music was never meant to be soporific.   Aaron Copeland

I BELIEVE WE ARE IN THE MIDST now of another enantiodromia, following the catastrophe of high modernism.   The situation music is in, as I outlined above, in theory provides an opportunity for a collective transcendent function to emerge. Rudolf Steiner, I like to note, commented that the future of music could fall to the English in the next century, now the one we are in, essentially a renewal from the periphery of the Europe wide project, a version of the renewing occurrences noted above, where the decline in one country preceded or paralleled emergent growth elsewhere.

However, music depends on audience, beginning with the composer's ear and widening out from there. Anything much more archetypally complex than the simplicities of the basic pop world, and indeed also of the so-well-known-that-it-has-become-anodyne 'classical' music broadcast on (UK) Classic FM radio, is beyond most people's willingness to thoughtfully appreciate: for that's where the mass market is, apparently needful, sadly, in our commercialised culture.

Though we should note that increasing 'cross-overs' in recent decades have revealed some rather more sophisticated popular music, which would seem to correlate with the well noted increases of more general 'awareness' in generations younger than mine.

More sophisticated music has historically required a more sophisticated audience and patronage, as exampled by Haydn with the aristocratic Esterhazy's in their palace in the marshes remote from the peasantry which paid for their ease. A partial contrast might be the Duke Archbishop of Salzburg, who seemingly had no real interest in music other than his aristocratic social duty to provide it, thus provoking the needed rebellion in the young Mozart—towards his musical maturity.

So pending a mythical future Golden Age wherein, despite the comment above, a larger proportion of persons are aware enough to appreciate and support developed music, and other arts, we will not see any truly pervasive resolution of the oscillation between simplicity and complexity which history shows us. Or perhaps the streams of so called 'classical' and 'pop' music will continue to move towards some kind of *rapprochement*. Though this, hopefully dreamed of or not, contradicts the tendency we have noted marking enantiodromic changes across opposites when a theme has run its living course.

Though I am maybe not being naive here with such longings: that age may already exist—in the next world.[15] Channelled reports from different times and places, and in differing languages and cultures, show remarkable correspondences, including attempted descriptions of the essentially

---

15 See for example Shushan 2022 and several previous books.

indescribable, seemingly truly transcendent music. I look forward to that ! My 3rd String Quartet came in a dream seemingly from some such quarter. I'm not sure, though, that I sufficiently matched that heavenly sonic dream into the elaboration onto score paper . . .

Sticking with what is still labelled 'classical' (which the elderly me comprehends) there may be some signs in this world, at least of seekings for the archetype. The Minimalist School of Adams, Glass and Reich, can hardly be said to have totally succeeded, but at least their work can seem a serious attempt to bridge the abyss between old dissipated diatonicism and the excesses (or incesses) of modernism. Arvo Pärt also shows a healing approach, as does our own Holy Minimalist, John Tavener. But it is not enough. Something deeper than re-workings of older ideas is required. But, but . . . the style itself should not matter: the individuation of the composer does, as in parallel Jung was careful to elucidate of alchemists in the context of his studies in the Alchymical work.[16]

Beethoven

SO, AFTER CIRCUMAMBULATING ROUND our subject, at last we find Beethoven. Here was a man searching to the depths of his being into the archetypes, bringing Promethean fires to the task, as his notebooks show. And in his so-called third period, now

---

16   Jung. CW12 §§40,448

only inwardly seeking, the struggle with the outer world of his second period no longer needed, perhaps he attained a worldly perfection in his music which very few can claim.

Thus the spiritual meaning of his deafness becomes clear, and in the last quartets we find him delving into music's origins with a tremendous spiritual, we might even say religious, passion (but importantly, without a creed) which is simultaneously profoundly calm and grounded. If he had not achieved his full maturity, his individuation, and expressed it in his last musics, then I do not know what individuation is.

He considered Quartet no.14 to be his most perfect work, but one needs to hear all of it, focussed, to appreciate its perfection—listening not to be done lightly. Instead, as a less extended reminder, there is the Cavatina from No.13, to which I am deeply drawn. This was recorded by the Quartetto Italiano half a century ago. Those four people worked together for many years, years of intense dedicated struggle to find the essence of the music they played: that struggle was etched into their faces, as portraits near the end of their time together achingly show. This is my preferred recording, a performance more deeply *real* than any other I have heard, which seems to reach the depths, in effect claimed by Beethoven by not expecting those late quartets to be understood until a hundred years had passed. And so it was.

These late works of Beethoven cry out in an intense feeling

to be heard, against a backdrop of T.S. Eliot's profound commentary on them, the Four Quartets.

I recommend listening to a recording of the Cavatina, preferably by the Quartetto Italiano, while reading, below, the ending of Little Gidding, and of the Quartets, and of this searching:

> We shall not cease from exploration
> And the end of all our exploring
> Will be to arrive where we started
> And know the place for the first time.
> Through the unknown, remembered gate
> When the last of earth left to discover
> Is that which was the beginning;
> At the source of the longest river
> The voice of the hidden waterfall
> And the children in the appletree
> Not known, because not looked for
> But heard, half-heard, in the stillness
> Between two waves of the sea.
> Quick now, here now, always
> A condition of complete simplicity
> (Costing not less than everything)
> And all shall be well and
> All manner of thing shall be well
> When the tongues of flame are in-folded

Into the crowned knot of fire

And the fire and the rose are one.

POSTSCRIPT

Once, listening to the Cavatina with some friends while we read the poem, a small cat examined us one by one as we sat down, and decided to jump to my lap, where she settled. I put a hand gently over her body, and noted that she was powerfully matching heartbeats to the rhythm. At the point the beat accelerates, her heart attempted to match the faster speed, but it was too fast: her heartbeats then instantly adapted to entrain with each two beats.

GLOSSARY

Archetype: Innate human potentials that are, or may not be, expressed in human behaviour and experiences, individual and cultural—see next term.

Collective unconscious: Contains the whole spiritual heritage of human-kind: they are patterns of behaviour and thinking which express through the archetypes similarly in differing cultures.

Compensatory function: Dreams as providing a balance to dominant conscious attitudes (differing from Freud's more constrictive definition as repression).

Enantiodromia: "The emergence of the unconscious opposite in the course of time." Opposites provide balance to any natural systems.

Individuation: The process of becoming fully adult, which may not complete until quite late in life, or not complete at all, depending on individual life experiences.

Jungian fourth: Based on the four basic psychic functions: sensing, thinking, feeling and intuition. Jung perceived that three parted constructs are common, and fundamentally unstable, requiring the balancing fourth.

Shadow: Archetypal instincts, desires, etc, repressed in order to serve cultural norm adaptations. Situates at the SM pole in Hill's model.

Transcendent function: The bridging function between conscious and unconscious, serving psychological growth, the individuation process.

Five

The archaeology of sound in ancient sites

WITH SOME THOUGHT AND PERCEPTIVENESS it is possible to discover acoustic resonances in appropriate places, without the intention to gather precise measured information, as have I in Scotland, just for the thrilling experience of the echoes thrown back directly at me, having placed myself at the focal point of incurved cliffs on the seaward side of Holy Isle off Arran.[1]

And on another occasion, on a visit to Stonehenge at a mid-summer sunrise, I had taken my tenor recorder, and played it standing against one of the stones, as the picture shows—it was the only place the sound was not snatched away by the wind. Or maybe it was in fact an appropriate place, for the leader of the group I was with told me he was moved to tears by my playing—an unexpected affect.

The leader was anthropologist Don Juan Nuñez del Prado, who energetically worked in Peru, Great Britain and elsewhere to preserve ancient Inca mystical practices, which were being

---

1   Only accessible at low tide: hence maybe not widely known.

ravaged and lost in Peru by the intrusion of 'modern' life. We had become close friends during his visit to the UK that year.

I had felt subtly honoured to be playing an improvisation in such a majestic situation: that surely had had an effect. But the picture shows that I was standing close to the sunrise axis, which perhaps was the real 'accidental' truth. For it had been ascertained at Stonehenge that sounds on the axis of the summer solstice were loudest and clearest—see below.

❖   ❖   ❖   ❖   ❖

THIS CHAPTER IS ABOUT SOUND RESONANCES discerned archaeologically among anciently built constructions, particularly but not only those underground or otherwise enabling echoes from offered sounds, leading to deductions concerning purposes and activities in ancient usages. This is a quite recent development in Archaeology. The discourse here is based on a review of the first book length survey reporting on this new direction.[2]

Since the Archeological discipline was established ancient sites have been extensively mined and studied for their visual aspects, as is apparent from museum culture, which is predicated on what can be *seen*. Indeed many words and phrases we commonly use as unconscious metaphors, like 'apparent', 'regarding', 'review', 'perceive', 'perspective', 'point of view',

---

2   Devereux 2001. Reviewed for *Music & Psyche Journal*. Here amplified and extended.

all connote vision: an example of the student affecting the studied, for we live in a predominantly visual culture.

In Archaeology, many references to aural life have been exhumed, principally objects perceived as ancient instruments, of bone or other surviving material. Until recently, though, no systematic attention has been paid to what has always been unmissable in Ethnology, that folk gathering for culturally important purposes also have ears and voices, and can play instruments, from drums onwards to more complex ones. Flutes made from bones are most likely to be found now, since organic materials such as hollowed out plant stems deteriorate: Newly found Chinese Neolithic bone flutes were reported as the oldest known in the journal *Nature* in 1999.

Paul Devereux, noted researcher and writer, with physicist and aerospace engineer Robert Jahn of Princeton University, investigated a restored 1000 year old Anasazi *kiva*[3] site in New Mexico, which revealed acoustic aspects, thus setting off the journey. They then moved to the UK and Ireland, in order to examine some older constructions there.

The remit of this field investigation was "to check the acoustic resonances of a small but representative sample of megalithic chambered mounds", including one of the oldest and largest, Newgrange in Ireland. But first, Wayland's Smithy was investigated, on the Berkshire Downs in England, north of

---

3   *Kivas* were darkened places for sacred rites, sometimes underground, reached via ladders.

London, followed by Chun Quoit on a ridge in Cornwall, deep in Englands south-west. In Ireland chambered cairns in County Meath were examined preceding the investigation of New-grange.

The work was done with the aid of sophisticated instru-mentation, to test the sought-for properties: resonances, stand-ing sound waves and so on, and to obtain detailed nuances of echoes and other sounds.

In order to put the acoustic archaeology findings into ap-propriate context, Devereux provides a discussion of ancient attitudes to sound, so different from the general modern atti-tude as being merely noise:

> Sound in the ancient world was conceived of as a supernatural phenomenon. ... If we think of sound only in the modern way, as a relatively inconsequential effect, we risk missing the significance of the new acoustical findings that are being made in archaeology today.

Thus we read of echoes as the voices of gods and goddesses, ancient oracles being often sited at caves, fissures and the like where amplifications occur.   Or evidence of acoustic considerations by the ancient builders of stone circles, burial chambers, temples and amphitheaters.

There are also chapters in his book on ritual and sound, and the effects of sound on the mind and body, which brings in perceptions of altered states, effected by entheogens and/or participation in collective rituals, including visions projected onto surroundings:

> when in a mind-altered state a person's perceptions become much more acute, so the swellings, depressions and flaws in rock-surfaces would have been more noticeable then during the normal state of consciousness." (p23)

These topics, though more extensively treated elsewhere, are needed here on the grounds that many potential readers drawn to the notion of sound at archaeological sites, may not be aware of the ancient and esoteric aspects of sound itself.

The work of various researchers are also noted in many different localities in the old and new worlds, in several different types of site. Here we find evidence of acoustic properties in prehistoric painted caves, for example as depictions sited at echo positions, which may also illustrate the echo, or stalactites perceived to have been hammered, emitting xylophone-like sounds.

The likelihood of the deliberate use of sounds in for example the Newgrange passage grave in Northern Ireland illustrates the level of discussion, with the fascinating possibility discussed of the use of smoke or steam which would take on visible structure induced by sound waves, however produced, illuminated by the ray of light entering the passage at the important ritual date. This could perhaps have seemed to those present then like the spirits of the dead taking on form.

Acoustic levels measured at various sites were found to be in the middle range of male voices.

Devereux also reports on investigations by researchers Aron Watson and David Keating from Reading University, which were occurring at the same time, the two teams unknown to each other until a paper was published by Devereux and Jahn.

Watson and Keating began with investigating odd acoustics at the stone circle of Easter Aquorthies in Aberdeenshire, and then moved on to the Camster Round passage grave in Caithness, Scotland, where, amongst other findings they found that the bass notes of drumming inside the grave, which at best could be heard about 100 metres away outside, created inside the related Camster Long, "about twice that distance away ... a subtle, distant 'booming' sound." They also considered that drumming at a particular rate which produced resonances in the monument could well have created altered mind states.

After that they investigated in Orkney, and eventually at the renowned and widely known Stonehenge, where they found that sounds varied in intensities influenced by the alignments and slightly rounded surfaces of the stones—clearly designed. The most loud and clear sound was experienced on the axis which points to the midsummer sunrise: an important finding.

One investigator just used voices, without instrumentation. This was Iégor Reznikoff from Paris, who with colleagues investigated some French paleolithic painted caves, in the 1980s, about a decade before Devereux and Jahn, and similarly before Watson and Keating. Reznikoff was aware of acoustic qualities in caves. He noted "there is no rite or celebration which does not use sound" and "the more primitive the society, the greater the quality of sound perception." An important perception.

They used tuning forks and vocal sounds. Reznikoff considered that a trained ear is of a precision unequalled by instrumentation.[4] As a composer and musician I am inclined to agree. His project was to determine whether there were relationships between sound and the paintings. He and his colleagues indeed found this, concluding that "the location of a painting was chosen to a large extent because of its sound value". This was also noted by Devereux and Jahn in their investigations.

And Reznikoff and colleagues also found that male voices were predominant.

Several other avenues of research in Mexico, Peru, and elsewhere, are also briefly discussed in the book, though the reportedly many old rock gongs found in, particularly, southern Africa, noted by Lyall Watson in *Lightning Bird*, are absent, not lying within the geographical areas investigated.[5] It is, though,

---

4   See *Ch.2* in this volume for another part of his story concerning sonic perception.
5   Watson 1982

a small book, and the author notes a number of earlier reporters on ambient sounds.

Since that book was published there has been and is ongoing work with natural sounds in landscapes, and also sounds 'guided' by defined structures: these are now named *ecoacoustics*, or *acoustic ecology*, or *soundscape studies*. And these have been joined by *bio-acoustics*, studying living organisms, from elephants and whales to insects. All of this has been enhanced by digital listening technology developments. All of this is extensively discussed in a recent book by Karen Bakker, in which developments in quantum physics are noted to apply to the subject as aid otherwise non-plussed explanations, a factor suggesting further study, not appropriate here.[6]

Paul Devereux is a respected writer and researcher on arch-aeological and ancient life-ways themes. His book is based firmly on discoverable facts, and the references are extensive. Nevertheless the writing avoids technicalities in the interests of 'the general reader'.

I was splendidly fascinated by this book, and by the BBC Channel 4 programme based on it, with which Devereux was involved. I hope many more enthusiasts will find themselves here.

---

6   Bakker 2022

Six

Hidden Faces of Ancient Indian Song[1]

READING THE MATERIAL WHICH GAVE RISE to this chapter brought to mind a lecture on Indian musicianship I had heard, presented by an Indian musician domiciled among the extensive Indian community in Birmingham, England, at the time of which I could have welcomed Solveig McIntosh's remarkable study, discussed here, as a relief to my feeling of dismayed inferiority that such intricate perception, as the lecturer presented it, was the purview of all Indian musicians.

The histories of ancient cultures should not be disparaged.

McIntosh is at once a scholar of and a practitioner in the ancient traditional music of Hindustan (North India), particularly Vedic chant. Her PhD thesis was entitled *Gamaka and Alaṅkāra: concepts of vocal ornamentation.* This chapter is based on a review of her later book, title used above, which advances from that thesis.

It is a comprehensive work, a revelation to Western minds of the intensely subtle development of the music of a very ancient, authentic civilization. The Preface states that the author travelled to India to find answers to the question: What creates the aesthetic experience in *rāg* from simple melodic formulas? The material she collected indicated that fuller answers required an investigation of the origins of *rāg,*

---

[1] McIntosh 2005. Reviewed for the Music & Psyche Journal: here somewhat rearranged and extended with comments from the present book's author..

Accordingly, via scrutiny of the complex (and notoriously obscure) Hindustani philosophical documents on Vedic chant and later, on music, some two and a half millennia of them, she examines pre-Yoga, pre-*rāg* systems, and how the various traditions—evolving through time, and also regionally—developed into the present day North Indian classical music theories and practices. During this journey her stated purpose expands, a change made perfectly clear in the Epilogue by a plea for a recovery of practices now discarded, or at least dimmed, to strengthen historical links with the "heritage of philosophic, esoteric and linguistic influences."

I took The term 'esoteric' here to refer to ancient purposes of inner change, of transformation, a reading confirmed in many places through the text.

Vedic chant is an example of a very ancient tradition apparently surviving remarkably by oral transmission alone, much as it was several thousand years ago—nobody knows how long. To this day Hindustani music percepts insist that the voice is pre-eminent, instrumental music an imitation. Indian musicians bringing their music to the West in the 19th century held that we would not understand their vocal practices, so brought us instrumental music first. Certainly true at that time of Victorian claimed supremacy beliefs.

The pre-eminence of the voice is an attitude perceived to derive from the sacred nature of Vedic chant—voices of the deities. This therefore brings Sanskrit into the discourse, as, among other treasures, it is effectively a vibrational grammar, which attribute attests to its great age.

This concern is in parallel with the equally ancient Aramaic language, which carries the essential *sounds* of spoken words, thus referring perhaps to some traces of the sonic origins of language which Steven Mithen masterfully investigated.[2]

McIntosh's book in some ways also forms an historical amplification, and so is necessarily concerned with the pronunciation of words and their sonic effects of external and internal resonances. These influence states of consciousness when done according to the ancient sources and the continuing oral teachings of the several variant traditions.

She establishes in her discourse a chain of connection from the ear through to *rāg* style, taking her cue from Alfred Tomatis' teachings on the primacy of hearing. Inner, or divine, hearing is considered equally important with the physiology of hearing, which she outlines, with a diagram showing a cochlea 'unrolled' for clarity.

Consideration of the mouth comes next, with the five tongue positions governing Sanskrit pronunciation. Very subtle positioning I find, rather like the problems of Chinese pronunciations, also requiring careful tongue positionings which are not in Westerners' early speech learnings.

---

[2] Mithen 2005

This leads naturally to consideration of the three Vedic *svaras,* implying accents in this context, arising out of original quite possibly level chanting. Whether these were just emphases or indicated specific pitches is not clearly established: maybe either, or both, in different localities and/or different times. At any rate some literature suggests a development into the commonality of seven tones dividing an octave via inflections of the three *svaras.*

Before discussing that, however, the author examines in some detail the tightly defined system of *mudras* (hand movements) which accompany the chants, with reference to the White Yajur Veda tradition (Mādhyandina Branch). These are held to have profound effect, compared to spontaneous gestural emphases of the *svaras,* howsoever authentically propelled from within. Arm movements are detailed, together with the precise holdings of hand and fingers which accompany particular final sounds.

Certainly inhabitants of that particular culture, versed in their ways, would have taken the hand and finger positions at the least as visual correlates of the movements of the chants. Thus the 'message' is strengthened by parallel modalities, vocal and visual. This and remarks above clearly show, in this and other authors' views, the negativity of mainstream claims that 'real' understandings are only possible by reductive thinking.

Armed with all that complexity, it becomes possible to

approach with some understanding the relatively recent history leading up to the present day nature of *rāg*. Octave species and tonal sequences are discussed as differing derivation systems, and then song forms and the characteristic subtle and gross sonic inflections prefixed and suffixed to tones *(gamaka)*.

Examples of Vedic chant patterns are given, which could be used perhaps as practice material, if the reader of the book has been attending closely, particularly to the pronunciation guide and to the author's careful discussion on the implicit intentions to produce resonances in the chanter's *cakras* (chakras) for the enhancement of consciousness.[3]

There are many valuable insights. This one, in her discourse on the subtleties of sound production from within the mouth, struck me particularly:

> It may be that the hiatus or 'gap' between the ending of a consonant and the beginning of a vowel is of ultimate significance. This is the 'gap' which can lead to perception of nāda brahman the original creating sound ... Those who study the texts of the Vedas may comment on the syllables and how they combine ... The aspect which is usually ignored is that behind all these units of sound ... there are gaps [in which] the mechanics of transformation take place. (p39)

Which reminds me of Itzhak Bentov's rather similar perception that, if we can notice it, the release from earthbound

---

[3]   Attending one of the authors workshops would be sensible, though.

consciousness is to be found in the pause between in-breath and out-breath.[4]

Some detailed consideration of the *svaras*, mentioned above, concerning what is present to be noticed between two sounded tones, reveals much complexity:

> In general, this 'sounded' tone, the *svarita*, occurs between the two others in pitch. It is formed according to the rules of *sandhi* (junction), by the most euphonious combination of two primary vowels already bearing separate musical accents. ... Depending on the way in which it is pronounced, each vowel has a particular vibration ... This means that the *svarita* accent possesses a particular vibration. However ... Traditions vary. ... Uttered alone it is an independent sound but in chant it becomes a glide. This glide is associated with a descending movement from the tone above to the tone below, [as was] the general tendency for archaic music to use descending melodic forms. (p47-8)

Indeed! A European example is found in ancient melodic calls for communicating across distances, such as a wide river, which start high pitched and wind down as the breath is exhausted. There are many old songs and cries, from France for example, which exhibit this pattern.

McIntosh notes that, with respect to the *svaras*,

> as far as the ear is concerned, the differentiation takes place at the level of nuance, a level of subtlety of sound awareness to

---

[4]   Bentov 1978

which, generally speaking, we no longer pay attention. (p48)

"We no longer pay attention." Not in our noise polluted culture!

Which brings us to the question of the *śrutis*, in which contention inevitably arises: Shrutis (to use the English form) are conventionally seen as twenty two subdivisions of the octave. McIntosh's discussion, perhaps necessarily, leaves loose ends. From the sage Bharata of c.200 AD she concludes that one *"standard" śruti* is equal to the Pythagorean comma (as it is known), the proportion $^{81}/_{80}$. Clearly this is far too small to be the standard *śruti* if one expects them to be equal sized through the octave.

One definition arises out of considering a cycle of perfect 5ths, which slightly exceeds in tonal extent a cycle of seven octaves, carrying the implication of a spiral movement. The small excess is often, and reasonably, seen as relating to the *śrutis*.

However Chaitanya Deva in his book on Indian music cites an English experiment which defined the least perceptible change of pitch as $^{31}/_{32}$ working out as about 22 per octave. He concluded nonetheless that *śrutis* are not equal in size.[5] And Alain Daniélou (a curious omission from McIntosh's sources) by detailed computation also derived from Bharata arrives at the theory that comma sized *śruti* intervals enclosed the seven uninflected divisions of the octave—therefore unequal sized

---

[5]   Deva 1981 p102

śrutis between.[6] This probably accords with actual traditional practice.

Hindustani philosophical history is long, prolix, and often quite obscure (particularly to us moderns weened on 'intellectualism'). The author's erudition, focus and energy in this field are evident in the dense press of discourse which this relatively short book contains.

But it is perhaps owing to that compression that here and there infelicities occur which leave at least this reader unsure of the writer's stance. For example in discussing scale systems and the harmonic sequence, she mentions that "certain select vibrations, tuned to the seventh harmonic (2 octaves and a minor 7th), have a neurological effect as they excite and amplify bio energies".

This would seem to imply the presence of a tonic drone for effectiveness, but maybe not, as the use of a drone seems to be a relatively late development in Indian practices. Are we in the relevant period? Does it matter for the particular point under discussion? The density of information and elucidation forgives. And in the current supposedly civilized world we need a drone to offset the persistent ambient noisiness which we all suffer.

A Guide to Pronunciation, the Sanskrit Alphabet, notes on the ancient literature and a Glossary usefully supplement the

---

[6] Daniélou 1995

discourse. I hope I have done justice in this review to what is, for all I have noted minor inequalities, a valuable addition to modern scholarship on Indian music, particularly, in my opinion, because of the author's careful and thoughtful attention to the reality of the spiritual aspects.

Seven

The Magic Flute – Die Zauberflöte

An illumination of Schikaneder's masterful perceptions

THE ELUCIDATION OF THIS TOPIC was perhaps for me an un-
balancing journey and maybe simultaneously an enlarging
thought bubble. Quite an illumination anyway. Or maybe not.
It sort of grew, like Topsy. And had me in a complex!

❖   ❖   ❖   ❖   ❖

WE EXAMINE IN SOME DETAIL, not Mozart's
music, but the characters and their interactions
in the plot. Gareth S. Hill's Jungian model of
flows in the psyche[1] is used as a structural
framework, which describes positive and
negative psychological progressions and relationships on a
figure of eight model. See Ch.3 *Flows in the Psyche* for an
exposition.[2] n what follows I shall use some abbreviations, as in
Ch.3. In order SF (Static Feminine), DM (Dynamic Masculine),
FI (Fiery Initiation), then SM (Static Masculine), DF (Dynamic
Feminine) and the WI (Watery Initiation), which is associated
with feeling lost, ungroundedness, being 'at sea', a sense of
drowning.

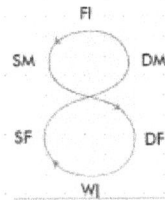

---

[1]   Hill 1992.
[2]   Or, for wider comprehension, the book.

The releasing Fiery Initiation (FI) is most often a painful necessity which probably all of us have to face at some time in life in order to achieve the next phase of our personal growth.

The Magic Flute characters between them evidence in their progressions through the story both positive and negative characterisations, and the important ones also developmentally progress, all part of the marvellously balanced story line, showing how perceptive of his fellow humans' characteristics and interactions was the librettist Emanuel Schikaneder, which validates Hill's model. This also shows that his understanding perception of these matters—however primarily intuitional—certainly precedently illuminated the work much later of C.G. Jung and others, by when perhaps the *zeitgeist* was ripe for their formally presented elaborations.

Here we go, beginning with the ...

Queen of the Night

NEGATIVE SF—The Devouring Mother, who expects all actions to flow back to her as matriarch. She is angry that her child is taken away—which was actually to allow the girl to grow, away from smothering motherhood (see below). That she is 'stuck' in the SF is underlined by her never *doing* anything herself. Hill remarks:

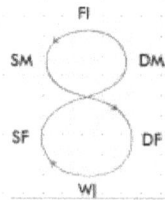

> When pervasive and dominant, each pattern represents its negative aspect, which in the static feminine leads to smothering entanglement, an inertia of snaring and devouring routine. Life becomes stuporous, a mere existence in the service of constancy, security, and predictability through endless cycles.[3]

Her shadow is in the opposite pole, the DM, which we will discuss below in the persons of the Three ladies and Monostatos. The Three ladies act for her, and she attempts to manipulate Tamino and Pamina, futilely in the end. However, she has plenty of fiery emotional energy, as her grand arias show, which we may say indicates the "dominant" quoted above.

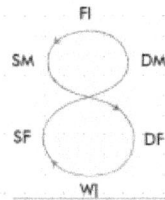

She is indeed the Queen of the Night, for the dark of the night time psychologically is equivalent to the unconscious, implying the absence of conscious development, which factor bears clearly on her inability to perceive Sarastro's true intentions and actions.

When I talked on this topic at a conference, an ardent feminist who was there was shocked by the description given above, angrily approached the dais from which I was presenting, and attempted to freeze me out of my 'masculine' impertinence, daring to present this powerful woman as

---

[3]   Hill 1992 p.8

negative, citing the power of her main aria as evidence. Deadlock! The talk progressed, though, and she saw the relativity of the point, somewhat reluctantly. Later we found some common ground in order to create a friendship—better than remaining pathogenically stuck with the animosity.

Sarastro

PRIMARILY HE IS IN the Positive SM as dramatic counterpart to the Queen of the Night. Here we have a struggle between matriarchy and patriarchy, but the dice is loaded by Sarastro's highly developed ability to be at any needed position in life, indicated in the psychological circuit. We may say he is well and truly individuated (fully developed in the Jungian sense). He represents the *benign* rule of order and structure, and his realm is essentially a spiritual one.

In this sense we may note that he also represents the essential message of the *Tao Te Ching*: rule yourself or others with wise power but not dominating force.

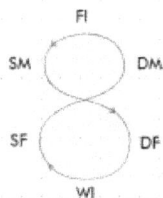

At the SM pole Sarastro's positive power and authority attracts to him those able and willing to suffer the Fiery Initiation. He is also able to be at the positive SF pole as an image or mirror of wholeness inspiring those who need it to grasp their own energy and autonomy and thus progress round the double circuit from the DM pole. So he is a psychopomp, which puts him at the positive DF pole. And he is also a man of action, occupying for that purpose the positive DM pole, shown when he is restraining Monostatos from killing Pamina.

Because he is easily able to be anywhere, his shadow is also everywhere, or nowhere, as he can freely move to wherever is required. And indeed no shadow is represented or personalised among the characters: perhaps he is an Elder in the fullest sense, the ideally developed mature being who has incorporated all experiences into his consciousness, and is thus able to guide and inform with wisdom. Certainly this is the central matrix for the entire plot !

The Three ladies

SOMEWHAT NEGATIVE DM—frivolous, vain, selfish and limited, as befits the expression of the undeveloped shadow of the Queen of the Night. They act out her dirty work for her, appearing deceptively positive when required. We may note the threeness, no transcendent fourth in sight which C.G. Jung would look for ! Maybe it's not Monostatos, as we might think, though he does seems to be their masculine counterpart.

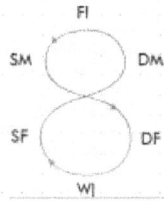

And we should certainly note what many commentators have put forward as the origin of these characters (and perhaps their behaviour too) Freemasonry: Threeness is pervasive in the

Singspiel, relating to its symbolic aspects. Nothing further here.

Monostatos

HE IS THE RAPIST, STUCK in the Negative DM, blind to anything but his own egocentric desires. We may I think surmise that Sarastro took him on as servant with the good intention of being a model for him of a more developed way of life, and to encourage him through the Fiery initiation.   But he resists any such attempt, remains in the DM, from where he can only reciprocate with the Devouring Mother, the Queen of the Night, as an aspect of her shadow. He is indeed in 'one state', as his name proclaims.

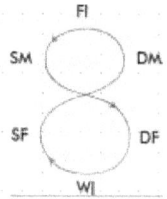

Hill's comment that psychological stasis, implying psychological problems, generally involves oscillation between two adjacent positions on the model, suggests that remaining imprisoned in one position would be far worse, a maniacally painful outlook !

At the end Monostatus and the three ladies are swallowed up in the Realm of Night, the darkness equating to unconsciousness. We may see this as a primitive SF, which is prior to physical manifestation—a hint of reincarnation maybe.

Tamino

HE IS OUR HERO, AND RUNS THE GAMUT. Hardly out of the natal

SF at first, his undeveloped self is therefore frightened by the snake, that chthonic imago, which fright he needs as the first stage of his necessary growth away from childhood. Then in his naivety he is deceived by the Queen of the Night (a false mirroring) into the role of the Dragon Slaying Hero, which he can fulfil only by attacking his own youthfulness.

In the end he traverses the entire circuit, and then round another half of it with Pamina, both of them having become adults with secure roles, so proceeding into Sarastro's realm, the benign SM, where the entire story ends.

Pamina

AND SHE IS THE HEROINE, also young and undeveloped at first. In some ways, her story is the more interesting one. Sarastro, who on the surface appears to be the despot holding her prisoner as claimed by her mother the Queen of the Night, may better be seen as the numinous masculine father figure who has removed her from the Devouring Mother in order to allow her space to grow.

From him she must be 'rescued' by the appropriate hero figure (Tamino in the DM position) who will take her round to the other polarity. In fact she does some of that work herself, in reaction to her mother's urge that she murder father figure Sarastro, and similarly reacts to Monostatos' threats, a fiery initiation which wakes her up: That is, she travels away from innocent childhood, constituting a move to the SM.

Then her despair on feeling she has lost Tamino owing to his silence during the air initiation (FI) drives her to the disintegration at DF, but the Three Boys prevent her suicide (her Juliet moment! and touching on the Psyche myth) and lead her through the Watery initiation to a renewed holism at the positive DF after a further complete circuit of our model.

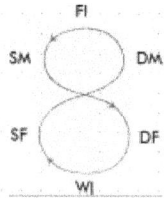

Papageno

THE DELIGHTFUL CHILD OF NATURE, he also begins from a position of potential development, but he has his own, somewhat more limited, but fluting! path to follow. The Queen of the Night sets him off (he reluctant) into a DM adventure by ordering that he accompany Tamino on the supposed 'rescue' mission to recapture Pamina.

Papagena

SHE SEEMS A SOMEWHAT CHTHONIC FIGURE, with a suitable nature as partner to Papageno. As the old crone and the young girl she stands at each end of a life cycle, both in the positive SF. That also provides a neat balance with the Queen of the Night's negative SF position.

Additionally Papagena represents the wisdom of the old

crone, standing instinctually at the DF pole as a disorienting factor which attracts Papageno (SM/DF polarity).

The Serpent

THERE IS AN ORIENTAL MYTH of a rich man without heir returning after death as a serpent to guard his wealth. Taking that as descriptive of the situation, young Tamino is scared away as a trespasser—which really means he is too immature, as noted above.

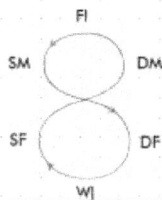

The Serpent, in addition to representing feminine consciousness as a grounded chthonic being, is also an animal symbol of the Dynamic Masculine. A point to note !

Being therefore in the Queen of the Night's shadow, which is probably invisible to that lady in her unidirectional being, her minions the Three Ladies kill it, which probably makes it a substitution in her thinking for Sarastro, whom she wants to kill out of hatred—she is unable to perceive his real being.

And so the Serpent points to the underlying male/female oppositions in the story, and therefore prefigures the positive outcomes yet to come, which will include the new unity of the, by then matured, Tamino and Pamina becoming the true heirs of Sarastro's spiritual kingdom.

Tamino's early and failed encounter with the serpent might be compared with the still immature Theseus in one version of the minotaur story 'killing' his anima figure Ariadne by abandoning her on Naxos.

The Three Boys, or Spirits

LIKE ALL MAGIC OBJECTS, including the magic flute and Papageno's bells, the Three Boys, together with various similar figures in other fairy tales, are morally neutral, in the sense that they will act for anyone provided the action serves the overall goal—development towards inner growth. As a species of higher consciousness they contain all possibilities as required, rather like Sarastro, so do not occupy any specific place on the model. They are the most developed other beings, in strong contrast to the Three Ladies, the least developed.

But they also are three. Again we find allusion to the three-ness structures of Freemasonry. Even so, they might perhaps collectively stand as the balancing fourth to the Three Ladies. Perhaps, though, in this saga the final actual outcome of the story is the real balancing factor to all loose contrasting ends. Rightly so.

The Initiations

THERE ARE SEVERAL OF THESE. Both Tamino and Pamina by implication go through both the Fiery and the Watery before coming together, both leaving innocence behind prior to their union: definitely an alchemical journey ! All four elements are in the initiations: Air in the 'not speaking' ordeals, followed by Fire and Water, which Tamino and Pamina go through together, each acting as psychopomp for the other.

And all take place in and on the Earth, which was hinted at in the initial serpent encounter, a chthonic figure, hugging the ground, the earth, which thus avoided the high flying tactics of Icarus, leading inevitably to failed collapse. So our hero and heroine successfully come through together, united: the alchemical *hieros gamos*. And the new day dawns, the *rubedo*, symbolising enlightenment.

Papageno finds the 'not speaking' ordeal, which he fails (of course!) to be fiery: it is noticeable that in effect he never leaves the masculine upper circuit on the model, and likewise Papagena seems never to leave the lower feminine circuit. So they find balance between them on the SM/DF polarity, this balance delightfully positive.

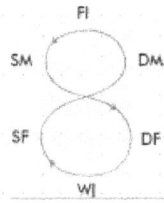

There is a musical magic moment when Tamino is about to undergo the water and fire ordeals. The two armoured men incant the Isis/Osiris ritual: 'endure and you will be enlightened'. Tamino declares he is ready, and from afar (off stage) Pamina's voice is heard singing the movingly simple line: "Wait for me!" And so we realise that she is the embodiment of his Anima, leading to the parallel realisation that he is the embodiment of her Animus. A perfect match: Wait for your contrasexual inner treasure !

AND SO WE NOW DRAW THE CURTAIN on this little digression through one of the best loved masterpieces of European music, showing hopefully how well its story relates to our human psychological needs and conditions, as an extended usage example of Hill's model of flows in the psyche.

Or was it, we should ask, not Shikaneder but actually that youthful genius Mozart himself who intuited the extraordinary perfection of this human spiritual story? Or was their collaboration a divine matching of personalities needing to find each other in the elaboration of this story, through which we all can perhaps find our own embodied myths?

Eight

Music at the Bauhaus, 1919-1933[1]

Four years of the Bauhaus are a chapter in the history of art. They are also part of social history, reflecting as they do the fermenting human situation of a nation and a period.

Oskar Schlemmer, *Diary*, June1923

The Bauhaus was a kind of school; but not a school that prepared its pupils for the world outside. Rather it was the other way round; that society went to the Bauhaus to unlearn everything it knew, to discover how to live in the modern world. Guy Brett. *Phenomenon of the Bauhaus.* The Times, September 20th, 1968.

The Bauhaus experiment was highly successful until disrupted by political catastrophe: it had a wide and decisive influence on the standards of design and construction both in Europe and America. Herbert Read, *Art now,* 1960.

IT IS A CURIOUS FACT that there is very little crossover between studies on the visual arts and those on the auditory. There are general cultural histories, to be sure, but even in those the two are generally compartmentalised, following the habitual trend.

---

1 This essay originated as an Appendix to an article on *Das Bauhaus*. This expansion of the *Appendix* was published in *Tempo* No.213, July 2000. Subsequent to Cambridge University taking over publication of Tempo in 2002, copyright of prior publications was reverted to authors. Permission for a translation into Portuguese was granted in October 2019 to the Universidade do Estado de Midas Gerais, Brazil. To date, nothing has reached the author from there, except silence. The essay is lightly edited here.

There appear to be few people who can think equally easily in or with respect to both modes, despite honourable exceptions such as Richard Arnheim and Raymond Head.

Yet there are grounds for thinking that music is intrinsic to the human psyche, starting with the obvious fact that, barring severe pathology, everyone includes music as an important component in their lives: the inference is that it is a necessary aspect of being human. But this is material for wider study, as exampled by Zuckerkandl, *Sound and symbol;* Blacking, *How musical is man;* Tomatis, *The conscious ear*.

The prejudices or compartmentalisms of scholars, however, do not preclude sympathetic regard among one set of artists for those in another mode. The Governing Board of the Circle of Friends of the Bauhaus included among their number Adolf Busch, Herbert Eulenberg, Edwin Fischer, Arnold Schoenberg and Franz Werfel, as well as architects Peter Behrens and H.P. Berlager, painters Marc Chagall and Oscar Kokoschka, and luminaries in other fields such as Albert Einstein and Josef Strzygowski. And though versatility among the visual arts was a noticeable feature of Bauhaus alumni generally there was at least one artistic crossover into music: the Dada composer Stephan Wolpe was a Bauhaus student first.[2]

Interest in the Bauhaus has fluctuated, as academic and cultural concerns are wont to do. The political situation erup-

---

2   Klemm 1989

ting into the Second World War naturally overlaid the excitements of pre-war *avant-gardistes*. With post-war reconstructions in the air in the late 1940s and in the 50s, supporters of the modernist ethos worked to point out the legacy, among them H.H. Stuckenschmidt and Siegfried Gideon. It was during this period that Hans Wingler laboured at his monumental collation of documentation, first published as *Das Bauhaus* in 1962.

The 50 Years Bauhaus Exhibition, funded by the West German state, came to London in 1968. This was a truly comprehensive retrospective, but more than that it sought to show current influences, and by also showing work by living Bauhäuslers, demonstrating continuity, perhaps succeeded. It was in some respects the cultural event of the decade, and generated wide attention, which issued in a burgeoning literature in the 1970s through into the 1980s: Clear demonstration of the perceived importance for 20[th]Century Western culture of the Bauhaus phenomenon. Several of the theoretical texts generated at the Bauhaus or by its influence[3] were then published in English, and also Hans Wingler's opus, in its third revised edition, in 1975.

This upsurge of interest came to a close in the mid-1980s with some critical reappraisals which tended to point up the negative aspects of the Bauhaus ethos, and the naïve idealism of its egalitarian attitude—an enanciadromicly appropriate criti-

---

3 Farmer & Weiss 1971, Franciscono 1971, Neumann 1970, Roters 1969

que from the right-wing political climate of that time. And when later more socialist, or at least centrist, politics once more took hold in Europe, it was seemingly time for a fresh look at this part of our recent cultural history.

After all it was not moribund: in household goods the firm of Ikea seemed to be a leading heir to the design tradition, and over the years we have all become familiar with the products of machines, good or bad. As I type, my work is lit by a young lamp whose shade was mass produced in the shape of a truncated cone extended at the smaller end by a tube. This design originated with the Bauhaus thesis, allied to the constructivists, of reduction to primarily three basic geometric forms: pyramid, cube, sphere. A pyramid, rounded, becomes a cone; a section through a sphere, extended, produces a tube.

At the same time there was a trend in this country (UK) towards house building with *kitch* parodies of 'traditional features' hung, or simply nailed, on the surface of brick boxes. It was time for a fresh look at the designed environment.

What is implied by these remarks is a study that is focussed on the arts of visual and spatial design. This note is not concerned with that, but takes a side glance at musical activity in that wonderful few years of the Bauhaus when a general desire among Germans for a fresh start after the First World War was focussed into a radical re-thinking of the ways of building and designing, overturning the 19th century negative attitude towards design by the machine, as held by William Morris and followers. My justification for this, apart from love of music, is the thesis stated above that music may be intrinsic to the human psyche. This is a preliminary survey of a piece of music history, if it can be so labelled, which, though there is much anecdotal evidence from many sources, seems not to have been written about specifically, except by H.H. Stuckenschmidt.

❖　❖　❖　❖　❖

THE BAUHAUS BAND

THE BAUHAUS BAND was formalised through time from *ad hoc* groups come together for dance parties and festivals (on which the *Bauhäuslers* were very keen) until from the mid-1920s it was famous throughout Germany, and a source of funding for the students. Xanti Schawinsky seems then to have been its leader. The band, he writes, was

> unified according to the rule of the art in a fantastically rhythmic and penetrating din [what else!]. Chairs, gunshots, handbells and giant tuning forks, sirens and pianos prepared by means of nails, wires, and any kind of tone-modifying materials supplemented the instrumental outfit,

which consisted by 1928 of some combination of banjos, pianos, bass (of unclear specification), trombone, clarinet, and saxophones. Schawinsky was the saxophonist and he also played the *flecaton* (flexatone?) and the lotus pipe (whatever that is or was), and was a 'falsetto tenor' (Schawinsky in Neumann). Anybody who could produce a near-musical sound was welcomed.

But what did they play? They were known as a jazz band, though the description above suggests something of rock (yet to be named), something of simple horseplay. Schawinsky states that the music played derived from the countries of origin of the participant Bauhäuslers: Germany, Hungary, Czechoslovakia, Poland, Switzerland, Russia and the United States:

> in its ensemble, from various folk sources or from home made composition [the Band] was able to produce guaranteed danceable music for hours. Improvisations, however, even when that threatened to get out of hand, seemed nailed together by the swinging sledge hammer rhythm (Schawinsky in Neumann)

Hans Wingler comments that they never practiced. And indeed, why should they, for the intended purpose!

In a study of 'Jazz reception in Weimar Germany', Bradford Robinson suggests that German jazz between the wars was necessarily home grown owing to the punitive cultural and commercial isolation that Germany was held in at that time. There was also an existing habit of looking, not yet to America, but to France and England, in matters of 'taste'. The earliest American bandleader in Germany, Alex Hyde, appeared in 1924. Various recordings which stimulated jazz in England and

France were not issued in Germany, and though an exchange system was established between the USA and Germany in the late 1920s, jazz recordings for German classical, the American system of segregated record catalogues meant that the 'race records' were excluded. Thus what we in Europe would now regard as the authentic jazz of that time simply was then not apparent in Germany. Even in France and England the recordings segregation was not much perceived.[4]

So the Bauhaus band jazz was an idea formed largely from rumour—as was for example Shostakovitch's, for similar reasons—and had little similarity with what the Americans were playing at the time.

But there was another influence noted by Robinson, the pre-war *Radaukapellen*, 'Racket bands' (the term was coined by George Grosz) 'creating jazz by disfiguring Wilhelmine march and salon numbers and peppering them with unmotivated explosions or sound effects from the drummer, and from police sirens and pistol shots' – something of which lives on in the opening to Weill's *Mahagonny Songspiel*. This clearly parallels Schawinsky's description. The Band was an expression of spontaneous youthful exuberance, rooted musically in existing aspects of German popular culture.

❖   ❖   ❖   ❖   ❖

4 Gilliam 1994 (contains no reference to the Bauhaus)

PAINTERLY MUSIC

AMONG THE BAUHAUS STAFF, the painters Wassily Kandinsky, Paul Klee and Lyonel Feininger had definite interests in music.

In his penetrating little study *Contemporary art in the light of history*, Erwin Rosenthal notes that Kandinsky's

> struggle for the 'spiritual' and the 'absolute' in art is reminiscent of Romantic aesthetics, and he is certainly in line with them when he states that the "spiritual" and the "absolute" can only be attained by sounds, by music. When explaining the composition of his paintings, he often used words like 'rhythmic', 'melodic', and 'symphonic'.[5]

The complementary view of Bauhäusler Will Grohmann was we suppose informed by observation at the time:

> Kandinsky took a ... theoretical interest in music, but one which was still intense enough for him to stage Mussorgsky's 'Pictures at an exhibition' with an abstract decor in Dessau in 1928. [He] adhered with an inner compulsion to cosmic order and legality, as did Arnold Schönberg, and therefore Kandinsky also found it hard to be understood.

Schönberg and Kandinsky were friends: Tut Schlemmer in Neumann. Unfortunately though, a check through published and easily obtainable works on Kandinsky and on Mussorgsky reveals no hint of that performance. Grohmann was perhaps misremembering, or remembering a rumoured expectation.

---

5   Rosenthal 1971

Kandinsky believed synaesthesia had a physiological basis but felt that stronger expression of his ideas could be achieved if the various arts could be used to produce contrasting effects rather than corresponding ones (unlike Scriabin and others who sought synthesis of, particularly, colour and sound). His belief finds support in some recent studies by, among others, Simon Baron-Cohen and colleagues in Cambridge,[6] though how far Kandinsky in fact managed to express himself cross-sensorially in his work, which was his aim, remains a much more subjective matter.[7]

Feininger had a point of "contact with Klee, who played Bach as passionately as did Feininger and had almost become a professional musician." (Will Grohmann again). Klee's violin playing is well known, and he is also remembered to have played in breaks from the dancing at Bauhaus Band events, along with acts from the theatre people and others (Neumann & personal observations in the *50 Years Bauhaus catalogue*).[8] Many fine students came to attend at the Bauhaus, but many left after the mandatory six-month trial period.

In 1923 the 'Bauhauswoche' exhibition was held just before the Bauhaus move to Dessau. Both were responses to hostile hounding by conservatives on the Weimar town council. This was the first public demonstration of Bauhaus work, and it

---

6   The Ch *Music making and healing the breach* in Bk1, discusses this extensively.
7   Lang 1980
8   Neumann 1970

gained international plaudits, at least from the cultural avant-garde. A number of musicians were there, including H.H. Stuckenschmidt, who was inclined to be condescending. He wrote in 1950, reminiscing[9] :

> As a representative of modern music, I was looked upon at the Bauhaus as a strange animal. Few links existed at that time between painters and musicians of the avant-garde, and modern painters like Paul Klee and Feininger, both of whom practiced music, had a most conservative taste in music. Feininger composed fugues in his leisure time and Klee loved to play Mozart on the violin.[10]

Klee also played Feininger's fugues (Walter Mehring in Neumann).

We need not assume that the above accounts for all institutional musical activity. There exists, for example, a photograph of Bauhäusler Joost Schmidt with a tuba, though whether he was actually a player is uncertain, as he is in some sort of party costume, as is the young woman on his other knee. Many Bauhaus photographs display similar artfulness.[11]

❖　❖　❖　❖　❖

CONCERTS AND MUSICAL EVENTS

OF THE MORE PUBLIC VARIETY of music-making there is

9　Reprinted in the 1968 exhibition catalogue from *Die Neue Zeitung*, 14.1.50.
10　Stuckenschmidt 1985
11　*Bauhaus Photography* 1985

some evidence, too. The 'Bauhaus week' of the 1923 exhibition included two concerts and two stage performances involving music, and the choices of composers was certainly not 'conservative' (Fig.1). Busoni, Hindemith and Stravinsky are remembered to have been there, and also Stefan Wolpe and Wladimir Vogel, though Krenek apparently is not (Naylor, & various in Neumann). Wolpe had been attending Bauhaus classes since near the beginning, and there wrote ecstatic piano pieces for the object of his desire. He and Stuckenschmidt maintained friendly relations from that year on. Stucken-schmidt's comments, quoted above, are worth quoting further:

> I was invited to participate.[12] We invented a "mechanical ballet" whose dancers were geometric cardboard figures, filing across the stage in rigid rhythms accompanied by my music. The initiator of the whole thing was a young construction painter, Kurt Schmidt. … Hermann Scherchen appeared and conducted Igor Stravinskv's "Histoire du soldat" with Carl Ebert as narrator.[13] Ferrucio Busoni was among the guests of honour.[14] Paul Hindemith conferred with Oscar Schlemmer about the 'Triadisches Ballett'. It was an entente cordiale of the artists of the future in which we saw a step towards a spiritual pan-Europe. [15]

12 Probably the only recording of any of his works, according to a reviewer, appear-ed on a CD 'Music at the Bauhaus: Steffen Schleiermacher plays piano music of Wolpe, Hauer, Vogel, Antheil and Stuckenschmidt'.

13 This was only the second performance, in the presence of the composer.

14 Busoni's health was fading at that time, and he died in the following year. See Fig.1, Sonnabend. The premières were four of the *Kurze Stücke zur Pflege des polyp-honen Spiels*.

15 Stuckenschmidt 1985

BAUHAUSWOCHE

MITTWOCH, 15. AUG.: 11ʰ vorm. Eröffnung im Vestibül des Bauhauses. 8ʰ abends. W.GROPIUS: Kunst und Technik, eine neue
Einheit / Vortrag mit Lichtbildern in der „Erholung" Karlsplatz 11.

DONNERSTAG, 16. AUG.: 4ʰ nachm. W. KANDINSKY: Über
synthetische Kunst / Vortrag in der „Erholung" Karlsplatz. Aufführung
im „Deutschen Nationaltheater" Schlemmer, Burger, Hötsel:
DAS TRIADISCHE BALLETT mit der Weimarischen Staatskapelle,
8ʰ abends.

FREITAG, 17. AUG.: 11³⁰ʰ vorm. J. P. OUD: Die Entwicklung
der modernen Baukunst in Holland / Vortrag mit Lichtbildern in
der „Erholung" / Bühnenwerkstatt des staatlichen Bauhauses:
Mechanisches Kabarett. Aufführung im „Jenaer Stadttheater"
F. W. Bogler, M. Breuer, O. Schlemmer, Kurt Schmidt, Joost
Schmidt, K. Schwerdtfeger, G. Teltscher, A. Weininger Musik
von H. H. Stuckenschmidt, 8ʰ abends.
Zugabfahrt: ab Weimar 5³⁰, Rückfahrt: ab Jena 11³⁵.

SONNABEND, 18. AUG.: 10³⁰ʰ vorm. Filmaufführung nach
einem vom Staatlichen Bauhaus zusammengestellten Programm
in Helds Lichtspieltheater, Marienstraße 1. Comenius Film-
gesellschaft, Carl Koch: Erziehungsfilm und Filme der Ufa-Kultur-
abteilung: Mikroskopische, Zeitlupen- und Zeitrafferaufnahmen.
8ʰ abends. Konzert im Nationaltheater. HINDEMITH, Marien-
lieder (Erstaufführung) Sopran: Beatrice Lauer-Kottler, Frankfurt a. M. / am Klavier: Emma Lübbeke-Job, Frankfurt a. M.
BUSONI: 6 Klavierstücke (4 Uraufführungen) am Klavier: Egon
Petri, Berlin.

SONNTAG, 19. AUG.: 11ʰ vorm. Matinee im Deutschen Nationaltheater: Leitung H. SCHERCHEN, / KRENEK: Concerto grosso /
6 Soloinstrumente und Streichorchester der Weimarischen Staatskapelle / STRAVINSKY: Die Geschichte vom Soldaten / Personen /
der Vorleser: K. Ebert, Berlin; der Soldat: F. Odemar, Frankfurt a. M.; der Teufel: H. Schramm, Frankfurt a. M.; die Prinzessin:
J. Petersen, Frankfurt a. M. und Mitglieder der Weimarischen Staatskapelle (7 Soloinstrumente). Wiederholung der Frankfurter-Erst-
aufführung.
Abends Lampionfest, Feuerwerk, 2 Reflektorische Spiele von
L. Hirschfeld-Mack, Bauhauskapelle und Tanz / Treffpunkt 8³⁰
Liszthaus, Belvedereallee. (Tanz und Aufführung in der „Armbrust"
Schützengasse).

Fig.1: Music & other events, Bauhaus Week programme, 1923

Modern painting and architecture became, so to speak,
official with the Bauhaus. The avant-garde theatre began to be
organised in Germany when Erwin Piscator and Bert Brecht
appeared on the stage. The first international festivals of
modern music took place in Donaueschingen and Salzburg in

the early twenties and composers such as Ernst Krenek, Paul Hindemith, Alban Berg and Darius Milhaud were heard in a renowned forum. The International Association for New Music, which to this day leads the promulgation of new, experimental, music throughout the world, had its beginnings in these festivals.

By associating developments in the theatre and in 'Modern' music with the Bauhaus, Stuckenschmidt seems to be inferring more than mere contemporaneity. This is understandable, not only from the point of view of cross-fertilization, but also as a direct consequence of the enforced social and economic isolation of Germany. Removal of restraining forces represented by active relations with settled neighbouring states provided the freedom and the opportunity for change, thus allowing to some degree leadership in cultural innovation to pass to Germany.

The dark shadow of that freedom appeared as the rise of the Nazi movement. Toynbee's dictum that civilization overrun by more powerful neighbours will give back in return new religious forms, as the only response available once indigenous cultural and economic mores are overlaid, seems to have found here in this case of national ostracism a powerful echo within the cultural sphere itself.

Another voice, that of Bauhäusler Kurt Krantz, avers that in 1930

I heard the musicians of the Leipzig Conservatory on the

> Bauhaus stage in Dessau. In the course of four evenings, they presented an introduction to, and an analysis of, contemporary composition techniques – eg those of Bartók, Stravinsky and Schönberg. [And, in 1931] the US composer and pianist Henry Caol [*sic:* Cowell], who presented his 'mechanic motion' with elbows and fists as an action. (Krantz in Neumann)

Who was sufficiently interested to stage technical analyses, more apt, we might suppose, for music students? On the other hand Bauhaus discussions among students and staff, which reportedly went on for hours and might be on any subject, could well have included comparisons with *avant-garde* developments in other than visual and spatial arts: it is tempting to suppose that these would have been stimulated, in that innovative questing atmosphere, by the visitors from Leipzig.

❖   ❖   ❖   ❖   ❖

THEATRE

THEATRE WORK AT THE BAUHAUS was extra-mural until the move to Dessau, where Gropius provided a theatre in their new building. Oscar Schlemmer, who had been lecturing officially on solid forms, was the energy source for this. He talked of the urge to perform, quoting Schiller's letters on the aesthetic education of man. Tut Schlemmer recalled that the theatre was

> first and foremost limited to silent action and pantomime.

Speech could be added later [This] also held good for musical sounds. Up to that time [1925/6] only gong and kettledrum were used.

Except for the famous *Triadic Ballet*. This was performed at the Bauhauswoche in 1923, with music by Hindemith.

The Welte mechanical piano was worked by punched paper rolls, and the music Hindemith wrote for his [*sic*] *Triadisches Ballett* ... was punched on the rolls with his own hand. Schlemmer had produced Hindermith's *Mörder, Hoffnung der Frauen* and *Das Nusch-Nuschi* at Stuttgart in 1921 and had then invited the composer to write a ballet for him. [The *Triadic Ballet*] was an abstract work proclaiming the triad as the beginning of the collective concept, as opposed to the individual (one) and the alternative (two). ... It remains something of a mystery ... Since the music was designed for and punched direct on player-piano rolls, it has not so far been published.[16]

Schlemmer describes the ballet as having originated in 1912, with a first performance of part of it in 1915, and the first complete performance in 1922, presumably after Hindemith had punched the roll.[17] The player piano idea certainly fits with Schlemmer's theories of abstraction and mechanicalness of movement.[18] (see also Schlemmer 1971)

In 1927 Schlemmer lectured to the Circle of Friends of the

16 Skelton 1977
17 Schlemmer. Moholy-Nagy & Farkas 1979
18 The *Triadische Ballett* reappears, aurally, in the additional music for the 2nd version of Stockhausen's *Momente* (1962)

Bauhaus. The lecture was illustrated by a written out choreography for his Gesture dance, a structured chart which somewhat two-dimensionally specified the movements from top to bottom of the page, with instructions for the musical effects at intervals down the left-hand side. From which it would appear that music for Schlemmer was part of a repertoire of sounds to accompany movement: dadadadada.

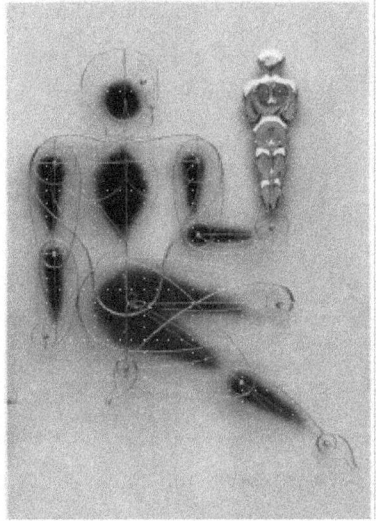

Fig2: Oscar Schlemmer. Wire figure

❖ ❖ ❖ ❖ ❖

INTEREST IN NEW MUSIC & COLOUR/SOUND THEORIES

REASONABLY ASSUMING THAT the reminiscences in Neumann's book are as partial as memory usually is, it seems inferable that the above were not the only interesting musical events to have taken place at the Bauhaus. Some person or persons was taking a definite interest in what was happening in new music. Alas, even the exhaustive documentation of Wingler throws no light on this, though he does note that a book entitled *Musico-mechanico* by George Antheil was listed among forthcoming

Bauhaus books in 1927, though it seems not to have appeared.[19] The presence of that item may imply a decision to incorporate texts on modern sonic art in the publishing programme, or it might be quite *ad hoc*.[20]

However, Stuckenschmidt, writing at greater length in the introduction to the catalogue of an exhibition on Music in 20th Century Art[21], points out that Johannes Itten, author of a still classic treatise on colour theory, who had started an art school in Vienna before he joined the Bauhaus, had there met among others Alma Mahler the widow of Gustav (later Gropius' first wife—she subsequently married Franz Werfel) and J.M. Hauer, with whom he made friends. Hauer's *zwölfton* theories were used by Itten as an extension of his colour theories, and therefore imparted to his students. Although Itten left the Bauhaus in 1923 "his thoughts on Hauer's twelve tone music were left haunting the heads of Bauhäuslers", in addition to which an elderly teacher, Gertrud Grunow, remained. She had become a friend of Itten's, and had developed somewhat similar ideas on the connection between *ton* (sound) and colour.

Such matters, avers Stuckenschmidt, also interested Ludwig Hirshfeld-Mack and Kurt Schwerdfegers. He also mentions Scriabin as being of interest at the Bauhaus, which one would

---

19 Stuckenschmidt recalls improvising in the style of Antheil (piano cascades) for Kurt Schmidt's Mechanical Ballet in 1923. See Fig.1 Freitag.

20 WIngler 1975 (1962)

21 'Musick am Bauhaus' in Vom klang der Bilder – *Die Musiek in der Kunst der 20 jahrhundert* (1985)

expect owing to Scriabin's interest in colour and sound relation-ships. "I found all these things in development in 1923 at the Bauhaus".

Written by a man in his eighties, there is a definite reminiscent tone to the article which suggests (perhaps I am being unkind) that clarity and verity may be blurred in the service of his preferences, but nevertheless there are some possible answers to the question posed above as to who was interested in modern music.

It may have been Gropius himself, who, apparently, exper-ienced music tremendously powerfully ("erlebte Musik unge-mein stark": Stuckenschmidt). This comment is perhaps paral-leled, or elucidated, by a remark made by C.G. Jung to pianist and music therapist Margaret Tilly who visited him in 1956: "music is dealing with such deep archetypal material, and those who play don't realise this". Many performances are thus essentially trivialised.[22]

Matters other than his work seem to have been scrupulous-ly avoided in other writings on and by Gropius. At the same time several well known musicians were associated at least socially with Bauhaus teachers, or Masters, as they were called. Schoenberg's friendship with Kandinsky, and Itten's with Hauer, have been noted, and Alma Mahler would have brought musical connexions with her in her marriage to Gropius. Alban

22 But see remarks by Philip Rawson on Pablo Casals and Josef Szigeti in *Time or Space*, Bk1.

Berg and his wife were also part of the same cultural circle.

There are perhaps inevitable attractions between prominent figures in parallel cultural endeavours, though this does not imply a necessary practice of 'modernism' in the complementary practice as Stuckenschmidt seemed to suggest in his 1950 comments, quoted above. Klee was entitled to his love of Bach and Mozart while no doubt being aware of newer musics, perhaps partly through his friend and colleague Kandinsky.

❖ ❖ ❖ ❖ ❖

MISCELLANEA

THERE IS AN ENIGMATIC REFERENCE to Bartók in the reminiscence of Marianne Brandt in the Bauhaus and Bauhaus People book. She refers to "pleasures of a different sort ... Klee playing his violin ... and Bartók". Perhaps he visited? Scanned biographies do not mention that, but it seems not impossible. (Neumann)

Inter alia the work of the student Heinrich Neugeboren may be noted. His visual representation of part of a Bach fugue is the most immediately striking outcome of the Bauhaus interest in synaesthesia (Fig.3)

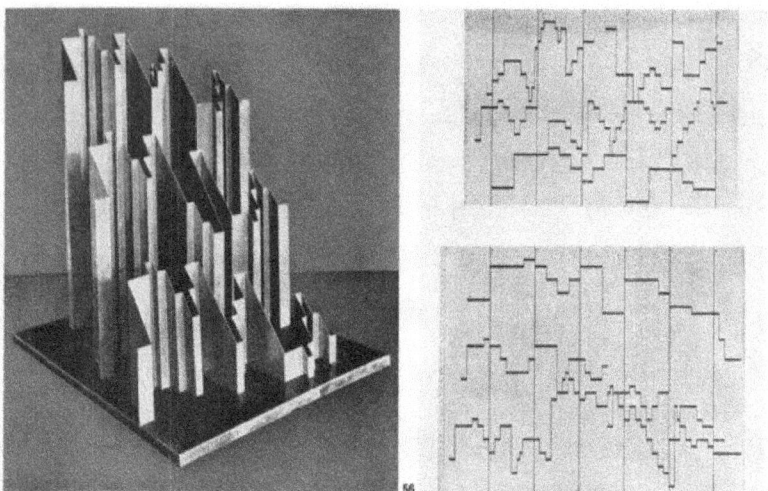

Fig.3: Heinrich Neugeboren (later in Paris calling himself Henri Nouveau). Design for a Bach monument, 1928. Four measures of the e flat minor fugue from the *Well Tempered Clavier* are represented graphically (right) and stereometrically (left, a replica in wood and cardboard by Gerda Marx). Neugeboren had his reservations: 'This kind of rendering so far represents an experiment. It has a disadvantage as it stands: the high number of vibrations of the soprano tones are represented by an appropriate spacial altitude in the corresponding plane. This high range in its towering monumentality smothers the bass.' *(Bauhaus Journal 1929. 1)*

And in conclusion, we must not forget Alban Berg's Violin concerto, dedicated 'To the memory of an angel'. Manon Gropius, daughter of Walter Gropius and Alma Mahler, died at the age of eighteen on 22nd April 1935, as Berg was planning the concerto. Berg and his wife were very fond of Manon, and so *'Dem Andenken eines Engels'*.[23]

POSTSCRIPT

QUESTIONS ARISING FROM the above are several, but are left

---

23   Kroher 1975

for another, fuller, study, requiring perhaps access to the city archives of Weimar and Dessau, and to other sources not approached for this preliminary study. Perhaps, given another high water mark in the fluctuation of interest in the Bauhaus, some engagement with the work may arise.

APPENDICES

1. Time and Mind: a brief appreciation

SEVEN YEARS AFTER HIS BOOK on ancient soundtracks was published (see Chapter 5) Paul Devereux, jointly with archaeologist Neil Mortimer, became founding editors of a new archaeological journal, *Time and Mind: the journal of archaeology, consciousness and culture*, which "should provide a forum for many disciplines and approaches, an interplay (as the subtitle implies) between explorations of archaeology, consciousness and culture."[1]

The first issue contained six articles, two of which involved acoustical considerations. Respectively: Richard W. Loose *Tse'-Biina-holts'a Yalti (Curved rock that speaks)* about a natural landscape shape which resonates from a focus point;[2] and Cook, Ian A., Sarah K. Pajot & Andrew F. Leuchter: *Ancient Architectural Acoustic Resonance Patterns and Regional Brain Activity*, whose title states the purposes of the study.

After seven full years Paul laid down the editorship, after Routledge took over publishing, as he needed to focus on other writings. Again, the mysterious passage of seven !

Having thoroughly enjoyed the book, I decided to subscribe to the Journal, and similarly found much of interest there too. As an explorer of sounds, musical and other, as well as a deep appreciator of the presentments of this earth we live on, and the marks left by us as a living part of it, how could I not?

---

1 Devereux et al 2008, Issue 1, Editorial

2 Rather like my Holy Isle experience, see Ch 5

2: Tuning, Resonance and Consciousness[1]

Thoughts and observations on the structures and workings which underlie our human activities, with some orientation towards musical sounds.

TWO THINGS ARE REQUIRED INITIALLY: definition of terms; and a structure for discourse. Webster's Third New International Dictionary states of *Tuning:*

> the act or process of putting in tune ... an adaptive influence or state of adaptation ... an act or process of adjusting with respect to resonance [applies literally to tuning radios].

Of *Tune (vb)* it has:

> to become attuned or receptive ... to bring into harmony ... to make responsive.

Keeping all that in mind (except for radios) we will also be concerned with the meanings implied in choices of pitch levels and relationships, specifically of tempered and natural tunings.

Also from Webster's, on *Resonance,*

> a vibration of large amplitude in a mechanical or electrical system caused by a relatively small stimulus of the same or nearly the same period as the natural vibration period of the system ... the intensification and enriching of a musical tone by a supplementary vibration ...

The word 'entrainment' will also be used to mean 'resonate', as

---

1 Written for a conference in the 1990s, it still seems to have some validity.

will 'coherence'—favoured in scientific writing, with the same meaning.

Consciousness as a concept requires more extensive comment. Webster's has this to say:

> awareness or perception of an inward psychological or spiritual fact: intuitively perceived knowledge of something in one's inner self ... inward awareness of an external object, state or fact ... the state or activity that is characterized by sensation, emotion, volition or thought: mind in its broadest possible meaning: something that in nature is distinguished from the physical.

This collection of thoughts lend me the sensation of struggle— as a tough etymological nut to crack !

Within science and philosophy a great deal of writing, and a great deal of controversy, has been emerging on consciousness. Only in quite recent decades hardly any scientist would touch the topic for fear of losing funding: Though now it would appear that the subject is moving to the forefront of concern. Before summarising recent thought on the topic, however, it will be useful to establish the structure for discourse alluded to above.

The great enterprise of modern science, held by the culture we live in to be the principal source of truth concerning the universe we perceive around us, established itself on the three principles of objectivism, positivism and reductionism. Or, the observer is impartial; empirically verifiable facts are the only reality (verificationism); and complex phenomena are explained by reduction to their components (e.g. genes held to explain all biology). Some, denying the spiritual, claim sole authority for science, with the probably un-thought constriction that 'science' only means study of the physical.

Various phenomena thus became difficult for science to deal with, not only the realm of the spiritual and the 'paranormal', which are extensively denied, derided and attacked, but also attention, volition, and other aspects of what we call consciousness. This should perhaps have been quite acceptable: there are areas which science is fundamentally equipped to study, and areas which it is not. But a tendency to grandiosity manifests as the claim that at least in principle science should be able to encompass everything. In common with that there is a strong philosophical tendency against dualism (material/mental, spirit /matter, etc.) and in favour of monism, the unity of everything. Webster's "something that in nature is distinguished from the physical" is a statement of duality. And there is a time/era dependency factor in science too, as the physicist Ted Bastin has pointed out:

> the very vision of the world that the science of a particular day gives you is heavily conditioned by what problems one can reasonably expect will turn out to be soluble given the existing methods and techniques ... that are available in that day. The areas of ignorance which are not penetrated, or at least not

> illuminated ... tend to be overlooked. Sometimes it is held that
> they cannot exist. [2]

And so we see the blindness which is the dark shadow of grandiosity giving rise to the all too common claim of scientific monopoly—what can't be measured, doesn't exist.

A way out of this difficulty in the form of hierarchical modelling has been suggested by several writers. These are in part a recognition that all scientific descriptions are metaphors, extending the finding of modern physics that a wave is a wave when it is not a particle, or vice versa, without either description contradicting the other.

Willis Harman, of the Institute of Noetic Sciences, has suggested a simple four level model, which I propose to make use of in this paper, as follows with examples (adapted):

level	health example	evolution example
4 .Suprapersonal	Spiritual health; wholeness	Universal purpose
3. Personal	Individual biological health	Individual purpose
2. Organism	Organ function; illness	Natural selection
1. Physical	Blood temperature	Molecular biology

Conventional physical science can readily be seen to be operating in level 1, with some biology and geology (etc) in level 2. Level 3 is occupied by the social sciences, and level 4

---

2   Encyclopaedia of Ignorance 1977 (Bastin)

currently by no 'sciences' recognized fully by Science (though transcendental psychology lays claim), but instead by religion and its affiliates. The purpose of the model, however, is to allow a structure within which, for example, transcendental hypotheses and statements can be validly attached to discourse in any science, and indeed that level 1 or 2 considerations can be recognized within any discourse held outside science, such as 'New Age' concerns about holism.

CONSCIOUSNESS

RETURNING TO THIS, our direct experience of consciousness is necessarily wholly subjective, since there is no apparent objective method by which I can discern your consciousness, nor you mine: external behaviour is not sufficient, since it can be argued that machines or zombies can emulate that, no more being needed, as transhumanists claim. We simply agree to accept that each of us is conscious. For this reason the nature of consciousness is a highly contentious subject in science and philosophy. Some attempt at a survey seems necessary therefore before moving on.

Daniel Dennett's denial

In terms of Harman's four level model there is a level 1 view which combines the 'objective' third person viewpoint with verificationism to deny any first person ontology: in other words subjective states are held not to exist. This point of view is represented by the philosopher Daniel C. Dennett, who argues powerfully in 450 dense, erudite, but nonetheless entertaining pages that consciousness is an illusion created by the functioning of our brains and nervous systems.[3] So perhaps I should puncture the illusion by refusing to recognize the pain of my toothache, about which I am all too conscious. Can't be done, at least not by me (a yogic sage might).

The pain is my own first person ontology, and I find myself unable to deny that philosophical category. Intuition insists that yearning for meaningfulness in life cannot be answered by agreeing to live as if my every-day commonplace experiences were only an illusion: the existential pain of that would be unbearable.

An epiphenomenon of the brain

And indeed Dennett's long time philosophical adversary John R. Searle argues that Dennett has simply denied the data. Searle, however, apparently on an article of faith, wishing to admit consciousness into the scientific canon as an aspect of physical reality, perforce regards it as something produced by the brain at a certain stage of phylogenetic evolution. This is quite an old idea, known as *epiphenomenalism* or *emergent properties of complex systems*, defended and argued by many,

---

3   Dennett 1992

though note that it contradicts reductionism to some degree. Perhaps we are moving out of level one.

But it leaves questions open. Just what properties of the brain are required? Reaching a certain size has been suggested, which children attain when language appears. But there are problems, not least the honours graduate in mathematics whose thoroughly investigated cortex is one tenth normal size, well under the limit suggested: he is not alone, others with similar physical brain abnormalities but 'normal' functioning have been noted. And just what is it that 'emerges'? If it is physical, where is it? No one has been able to point to any location in the brain or elsewhere and say 'there is consciousness'. If it is not physical, are we not in dualism?

Searle wishes to reject the old categories of materialism and dualism (mind/matter) in favour of accepting that

> consciousness is both a qualitative, subjective "mental" phenomenon, and at the same time a natural part of the "physical" world.[4]

In other words, he wants to force it back into level one. At the same time, he seems to have substituted a new dualism for the old. But it is a step forward from denial, albeit still reductionist. What neither of them take account of in their books are the findings of quantum physics. The topic is mentioned in Searle's book, but only as part of his review of the thinking of the

---

4   Searle 1997

mathematician Roger Penrose on consciousness, who argues from Gödel's theorem that:

> -- consciousness is not computable (cannot even be simulated on a computer)
>
> -- neurons are objects explainable by classical physics and therefore computable
>
> -- therefore neurons are the wrong level to produce consciousness
>
> -- at much finer levels within neurons are structures called micro-tubules which are on the edge of having quantum mechanical properties: here is the source of consciousness (provided that a non computable quantum mechanics can be developed).[5]

This resolves down to yet another materialist account, differing only by being reductive to finer levels than that of others. But he may well be right concerning quantum mechanics.

THE QUANTUM PHYSICS UNIVERSE

THE *MYSTERIOUS* **FINDINGS** of quantum physics have been seen by several as describing a quite other universe than the universe of classical physics, though maybe better to see it as an *extension*. In the words of astrophysicist Victor Mansfield:

---

5   Penrose 1994

First, quantum mechanics is radically acausal ... individual events do not have well defined causes. *It teaches us that lawfulness in nature does not require causality* ...

Second, objects in quantum mechanics cannot always be localized in finite regions of space and time ...what happens in a region, say at one end of the lab, instantaneously affects what happens at the other end ... There is no energy or information exchange ... *Non-locality teaches that the relationship between parts is more fundamental, more real, than the isolated identity of the parts* ...

Third, quantum objects do not have well-defined properties independent of observation ... they are [also] intrinsically indeterminate prior to observation. In other words, *we must participate in defining the world through our observation.*[6]

Quantum physicists have concluded that not matter but space should be regarded as the primary reality, because of the discovery of an underlying filled plenum known as the physical vacuum, the 'fine' or 'subtle' world, or the 'quantum vacuum', not actually empty, but filled by

an intense energy known as the 'zero-point field'. In itself this vast field is not electromagnetic, gravitational or nuclear. Instead it is the originating source ... The energy density ... is well-nigh inconceivable ... greater by far than the total matter density of the universe ... it is what physicists call 'virtual' or negative energy ... however, a region ... can be kicked from negative into positive energy, and so give rise to matter ... light

---

6   Mansfield 1997

> and sound are traveling waves ... rocks and swallows, and
> other seemingly solid objects, are standing waves in it.[7]

In Russia Akimov and associates considered that all objects, from quanta to galaxies, create vortices in the quantum vacuum. These are described as torsion waves, and are not only real, but long lasting. The plenum is considered to be in essence an information field, and the torsion waves capable of transmitting information almost without energy and at speeds which are multiples of that of light, thus transcending that limit in Einstein's universe. This, to take but one example, may explain the 'instantaneous' effects in quantum particle experiments, but more to the point of the present discourse is the idea that consciousness is embedded in a web of relations in the zero-point field:

> The emerging insight is that our brains can receive inform-
> ation not only through the five senses, but also by tapping
> directly into the waves in the vacuum field ... Everything that
> goes on in our minds leaves its wave-traces in the embedding
> vacuum field, and our minds are constantly receiving the
> subtle patterns that propagate there.[8]

These receptions are usually unconscious, but in certain altered states of consciousness information from other than the senses and personal memory can be discerned. Studies of near death-experiences (NDEs), regressions via relaxation techniques

7 Laszlo 1997
8 op. cit.

to past life events providing conscious knowledge which clears up present life problems, study of human body field effects after biological death, and the now hopefully regarded-as-'respectable' studies in psi/esp phenomena,[9] all seem to point, not only to the existence of consciousness operating independently of the physical body, but in the light of remarks quoted above, to vindication of C.G. Jung's insight concerning the collective unconscious, seen by leading edge physics to be rooted in the quantum vacuum:

> The most important result of the investigation is the understanding of the integral physical nature of human Consciousness as a manifestation of highly organized field matter (the primary torsion fields), the Physical Vacuum of the Universe and, particularly, Universal Consciousness.[10]

This vision of the unity of all things reflects the assertions of what Huxley called the 'perennial philosophies', the contemplative traditions underlying all religions, but most evident in the orient in, for example, Buddhism. We have arrived at level four description, to which we shall return.

In current western philosophical thinking it should be possible now to discern unity in the plenum, and to accept duality at the derived level of consciousness (or mind) and matter. The implied relationships may be modelled with a möbius strip, one side becoming the other, the other becoming

---

9   Lorimer 1990; Woolger 1990; Korotkov 1996; Targ 1984
10   Akimov (i) 1996

the one. Meanwhile, for present purposes it is not necessary to choose *which* model of consciousness in order to proceed. We may be able to shed a little light on the issues in due course.

THE BODY VIBRATORY

Physics and chemistry

THE TRADITIONAL SCIENTIFIC CONCEPTS that the body is composed of pieces of matter which act together mechanistically are hopefully being replaced by newer concepts of energy inter-relationships in part derived from quantum mechanical findings. We know from the study of atoms (from which everything physical is conventionally held to be constructed) that at that level there are vast spaces. This may be grasped by picturing a hydrogen atom nucleus as one millimetre across: the circulating electrons, etc, would then be at a distance of ten metres. In between is vacuum, filled by by an intense electro-magnetic field holding the system together, which radiates out to affect adjacent atoms. They vibrate at enormous rates, causing the molecules they make up to vibrate coherently both mechanically and electro-magnetically, but at a lower rate.

Molecules emit, therefore, sound, and light in the ultra-violet range (UV), but both of very low intensity. The photon emission is mitogenic (induces cell division). There may be a communication system between cells based on structures found in all cells called microtubules, which resonate in the range of the UV.[11]

Spectral analysis of that UV emission indicates that the molecular levels of living systems must be in a state of *far from thermodynamic equilibrium*.[12] The Russian chemist Ilya Prigogine won his Nobel prize for work on *far from equilibrium dissipative systems*. He showed that such open systems, performing in equilibrium according to reductionist science, when forced from that state became chaotic and then spontaneously generated new structures, not apparent before—order emerging out of chaos (contradicts reductionism). This was noted in experiments with living system molecules and has been known for some time as perhaps the most important emergent property of living systems.[13] We are moving to level two description:

> there is much experimental evidence showing that organisms respond to extremely weak artificial electromagnetic sources. In many cases organisms are so sensitive that they respond to signals below the threshold of thermal noise ... it is necessary to think of [this] in terms of transfer of information. It implies that the living system must itself be organized by intrinsic electromagnetic fields.[14]

---

11   Wilson 1997
12   Voeikov 1996; Ho 1991
13   Cottrell 1977
14   Ho & Popp 1991

This suggests that, for example a liver cell, vibrating at its own resonating frequency, will entrain with surrounding cells, also liver, and thus a field will be produced which is characteristic of 'liver', within which, in the healthy state, new cells will be constrained by resonance to develop to the 'liver' model.   This is called morphogenesis, Rupert Sheldrake's hypothesis, slowly acquiring acceptance in orthodox science.

Thus we see a system of interlocking electromagnetic vibratory fields in the body. These step down in frequency with increasing mass, according to Itzhak Bentov:

> -- the atomic nucleus is vibrating at 10 billion (English)
>   gigaHz,
>
> -- the atom at 1 million gigaHz,
>
> -- molecules at 1 gigaHz (or 1,000megaHz)
>
> -- cells at 1 kiloHz (or 1,000Hz)
>
> -- organs at ? [varies with organ size?]
>
> -- whole body length 375Hz

Clearly these are in resonant relationships: 375 is 250 X $^3/_2$ (its musical 5th), and 250Hz is two octaves below the cell vibratory rate. (More on this below.)

Nerves and brain

Overlaid on those, derived from fundamental atomic vibrations, are the nervous system rhythmicities. Sensory nerve cells fire at similar rates: rather randomly when in an unstimulated state, but when stimulated, they fire in bursts at rates varying according to the strength of the stimulus. If the stimulus (say, a sound) is at low intensity the rate will be up to about 200Hz, but this can be forced up to perhaps beyond 300Hz if the intensity increases. However the bursts will now be shorter and rest periods before the next firing will be longer: the higher and longer the intensity the more likely the nerve fibre will be permanently damaged (look at the sun; listen to the over amplified band too long!). It is supposed that in order for the ear to process sounds of pitches higher than 300Hz, nerve fibres cooperate to fire in relays, the overlaps producing by their sum the representation of the higher vibration rate.[15]

The brain, as is well known, produces from its own activity a range of electrical frequencies, associated with broad bands of differing conscious states. These waves are generally classified as follows:

> -- Beta- wide awake state, awareness focussed externally, 13-30Hz (or more)
>
> -- Alpha - relaxed wakefulness (inhibited by sensory stimulation) 8-13Hz
>
> -- Theta - near sleep, daydreaming, or in meditation, hypnagogic state 4-7Hz
>
> -- Delta - deep sleep 0.5-4Hz

---

15   Bentov 1978

The important factor in this for present purposes is that a feedback system appears to be present between the brainwaves and bodily conditions, which also affects the mind (consciousness). Each can affect the others, and do all the time. We can lower our brainwave rate by consciously relaxing the body, with consequent change in consciousness, or we can lower our brainwave rate by biofeedback or meditational (relaxing the mind) techniques, and our body will relax, though actually the events tend to happen together. This is a mind/body integrated system.

RESONANT SYSTEMS

THE UNIVERSE IS PACKED with resonance. Wherever there is rhythmic (which includes circular) movement there appears to be a tendency for relationships of vibratory rates to occur, resulting in entrainments. This results in energy conservation, since an entrained system requires less energy to continue than do the parts operating separately. Importantly, where two linked energies differ slightly in their vibrational rates (or proportional rates) the faster will usually force the slower to match speed.

Examples of entrainment abound. We ourselves are governed by the cycles of the moon and of night and day, as the jet-lag effect testifies. Women living together have been noted to entrain their menstrual cycles, as noted. Fireflies in a bush will tend to coordinate their winking. Our planetary system is partly the product of resonant adjustment: we may recall Kepler's insightful calculations that planetary distances correspond to musical harmonic proportions. Joachim-Ernst Berendt's *Nada Brahma* contains a wealth of examples and discussion on this topic.

In addition to simple resonance created by two waveforms with the same wavelength, we must bear in mind the resonant relationships created by waveforms which differ in their wavelengths according to whole number fractions, that is, according to the harmonic series. These relationships appear to be pervasive in the universe. An example is in the atoms most decisive for the development of life—oxygen, nitrogen, carbon and phosphorus: harmonic relationships are found in each.

In oxygen, for example, there are eight electrons, whose spin rates precisely parallel the whole steps and half steps of the western major scale, which is also an ancient modal scale. Matching the electrons are protons of the nucleus, organizing themselves in seven of twelve possible positions (note the seven pitches of a diatonic scale, out of the twelve full set of semi-tones). In the carbon atom a similar analysis reveals the equivalent of the pitch relationships of the Greek tetrachords— all three, depending on the saturation state of the atom.[16]

Coherence in the body

---

16   Berendt 1988

A number of the rhythmical systems in the body are susceptible to resonance. Bentov, using a sensitive seismograph-like instrument, was able to identify a number of tuned rhythmic oscillators. A pulse in the aorta, the largest artery in the body, is initiated by blood expelled from the left ventricle of the heart. This creates a pressure wave which travels down the aorta and is partly reflected back up by the aortic bifurcation (where it splits to go down each leg).

If in the meantime the heart ejects more blood, and a new pressure pulse is traveling down, then the two pressure fronts will eventually collide somewhere along the aorta and produce an interference pattern.[17]

Seemingly a counter rhythm produced by breathing has a strong effect on this system, for if we hold our breath, or enter a meditational state, in which breathing becomes much shallower, the heart will entrain with the aortic pulse such that the ventricle waits for the reflected wave to return before ejecting more blood. Thus they become a resonant system, which sets up a standing wave of around 7.8 Hz. This is a mechanical vibration of some power, and the body reacts to it, creating rhythmic micro-movement in the tissues and the skeleton. As a consequence an up and down movement of the brain is induced in its cushioning fluid, resulting in reverberating acoustic waves of 1000Hz through the brain.

17   Bentov 1978, 27

These waves in turn create standing waves in the ventricles of the brain, in octave relationships.[18] Seven octaves down from 1000 Hz is a fraction over 7.8Hz: the aortic standing wave will be induced to resonate at 7.8Hz. The entire system is resonating.

Assuming that we are in fact in deep meditation while this systemic mechanical resonance is establishing, we need now to note that our brain waves have reduced with our change of conscious state, and we are on the border between Theta and Alpha. Researchers have found that when experienced meditators report the feeling of 'oneness-with-all', their brain waves are around 7.8Hz (reference mislaid). We now have a mechanical (acoustic) and an electromagnetic resonance. Sound vibration differs from electromagnetic vibration in *displacing* the medium of transmission, whereas the latter propagates by changes in the electromagnetic field intensities in the medium.

Is there a connection between the two types of vibration?

We know that piezo electric phenomena occur strongly in quartz crystals (and in all matter, but generally very weakly) enabling a conversion from mechanical pressure to electro-magnetic energy.[19] There are in fact a number of crystalline structures in the body, having similar properties to quartz, such as liquid crystals in the blood, salts in fatty tissues, colloidal structures of the brain, the pineal, and crystalline bone compon-

18   Bentov 1978. 26/8
19   Gladzewski 1951

ents.   They will probably act as amplifiers of particular frequencies, as does quartz.[20]

In addition there is a substance called melanin, or neuro-melanin, in and around the brain.   This substance is a trans-ducer, and will transduce sound into light.   Neuromelanin is found in the pineal gland.   The pineal is in the brain but not of it, being outside the blood/brain barrier.   Nevertheless it will be moved by the mechanical, sound inducing, entrained vibrations in the brain, and thus stimulated to produce neuromelanin, which triggers the release of a substance containing phosphorus.

The resultant light emission, as well as helping entrainment with the brain waves, will enhance the bodies' electrostatic field (aura):   if intense enough, we will glow in the dark—only per-ceivable, though, in absolutely *total* darkness !

All of these would seem capable of converting at least some components of the mechanical vibrations noted above, and therefore entraining both systems.   There is melanin elsewhere, too, such as in the heart, which may well also play a part.   The sound transducer in the ear will be considered below.

Now we have a level three picture of a human organism as a resonant field of sound and electromagnetic (including light) vibrations, pulsing out into the environment, the mechanical

---

20   Wilson 1997

propagating so far, the electromagnetic much further, since the wavelengths are far longer. How do we relate out there?

Resonating with the universe

The influence of the moon and diurnal rhythms was noted above. There are other influences. For present purposes the Schumann Resonance is startlingly relevant. The ionosphere is well known to be a reflector of radio waves, therefore important for modern communications. It is in fact an electrically charged layer, the positive end of a capacitor the negative side of which is the surface of the earth. The potential difference is about 200 volts per metre, and this results in a standing wave of 7.8 Hz, the figure arrived at for the totally resonating body/mind. This may be the fundamental frequency of life,[21] if so this resonating field cannot be done without. NASA found it necessary to include an artificial Schumann resonator in space capsules, or the astronauts got sick.[22]

So, the experienced meditator enjoying the mystic vision of 'oneness with all' is in plain fact coupled with the environment in a resonating system. And more than that, for the wavelength of that 7.8Hz electromagnetic resonance is very long, nearly 40,000 kilometres, near half the circumference of the earth. Such a wave will penetrate everything natural, travelling round

21   Bentov 1978. 38ff
22   Wilson 1997. Note, 2020/21: recent measurements of the Schumann Resonance noted that occasionally it rose in parallel with global anxiety levels of brain vibrations.

the world about eight times a second. This means that meditators everywhere are resonating with each other.

We are indeed in level four description. Is this picture an aspect of the more 'mystical' interpretation of the Gaia hypothesis? The vibrational resonances extend out into space, too, but for the purposes of this paper we must leave them . . .

SOUND, STRUCTURE, CONSCIOUSNESS

HAVING EXAMINED VIBRATIONS as it were from the inside of the organism out, we now reverse this and take a look at matters from the point of view of sound penetrating inwards.

Sound creates matter

In the 1800s Ernst Chladni placed powders on thin metal plates which he vibrated with a violin bow, whereupon the powders moved into ordered patterns, varying with the place of bowing. This work was followed up a century and a half later by the Swiss scientist, physician and artist Hans Jenny, who constructed a more sophisticated device for studying the effects of sound which he called a tonoscope. He named his work Kymatik from the Greek for 'wave' (in English Cymatics).[23]

Biologist Lyall Watson has noted that Chladni's figures are frequently redolent of familiar organic forms,[24] and researches

---

23   And see p38 in Ch.2 for more recent work here.
24   Watson 1974

at the Cymatics Institute amply confirm the meaningfulness of the sound induced shapes. The vowel 'O' intoned into the machine creates a ring shape; spoken letters of Sanskrit and Hebrew (but not alphabet based tongues) reportedly produced the written forms of those letters, and many sounds produce shapes strikingly similar to biological forms, and processes such as cell division, for the impelled shapes are not static, but continuously rein-forcing themselves while the sound lasts.[25] the written formations are challenged by some[26];

Sound and music in the body

If sound will *create* forms of matter, it should also be capable of *affecting* existing matter. And so it does. The author was privileged a few years ago to see a sequence of photographs showing human cells deforming under the impact of differently pitched tones produced on standard musical instruments.[27] The experiments were done by Fabien Maman, musician, bioenergetician and martial artist, with the help of a trained biologist. These have now been published, but rejected by orthodoxy.[28]

---

25 Jenny 2001
26 Goldman, among others: my memory is of seeing photographic evidence of this many years ago, but the source is no longer apparent. It is possible that earlier publications of Jenny's may have such photographs (not seen). The English edition of Cymatics cited here does not, which claims to be the complete original 2 vols in one binding. Recognizable vowel forms *are* in the book.

27 Including cancer cells: legally in the UK I am forbidden to make any such 'claim' . . . *vide* 1939 Law. Maman 1997.

28 Further information on Fabien Maman is in Ch.2 in this volume, p39

However, those were outside their normal context. In the body, the normal routes for reception of sound are the ears, via bone conduction, and, Dr Alfred Tomatis considered, the skin as well. Sound is carried into the inner ear as physical energy. There it enters the cochlea, where the vibrations are converted into electrical nerve impulses, another piezoelectric effect. The nerve impulses are carried along the auditory nerve to the thalamus which is situated on top of the brain stem. The thalamus receives all incoming sense data (in electrical form) and sends it to appropriate parts of the cortex. Around the thalamus is the limbic system, which is believed to play a role in organizing our emotions, and also interacts with the endocrine glands, influencing respiration, pulse, blood circulation and hormonal secretions.[29] It is in these areas that we may expect finer understanding of the way in which sound and music affects us, physically and emotionally, and possibly of spiritual affects too.

That it does so affect us is to an extent obvious, as well as inferred from discussions above. Strongly rhythmic music, especially if loud, energises. Soft airs lacking in emphasised beats will likely relax. Music brings about similar physical responses in different people at the same time, and the making of music is firmly rooted in the body. Music causes arousal, that is, heightened alertness, awareness, interest, and excitement: a generally enhanced state of being.

29   McClellan 1991: 24*ff*; Campbell 1992: 26*ff*)

Much work has been done on brain electrical activity related to various tasks. Two examples concerning music will suffice here. Petche and colleagues in Vienna have measured multiple coherences across and within both brain hemispheres during such tasks as listening to music, mental arithmetic (as a comparison), imagining known music (a performer), score reading and mentally composing. Coherence across the brain is increased during all musical tasks, particularly composing. Brain laterality as well as coherence varied according to individual interest in or knowledge of the music, and according to *level of attention* (Petche).[30]

Frances Rauscher and associates in the University of California caused a stir in 1993 when they published findings that listening to Mozart enhanced abstract reasoning. Clearly the brains of subjects were being energised. However the effect noticed was temporary, and the study was rather limited, which they noted (Rauscher). Nevertheless, despite that careful scientific caution, the effect seems to be real. Sales of Mozart recordings rocketed, rather amusingly, as other fine musics have similar effect.

Physico-chemical changes in the body correlate with thoughts as well as emotions. There *is* a biology of hope, fear, optimism, guilt, self esteem, love ... And as we saw in the case of the meditational state, bodily changes accompany changes in

---

30   Petche 1993

states of consciousness. It is possible that the feedback system between the brainwaves and the body, mentioned above, together with the correlations between body and thoughts/emotions, may in fact be powered (if this physical energy term is allowed) by *meaning*, as has been suggested by physicist David Bohm in his theory of *soma significance*: the role of meaning in how reality unfolds for us. He proposes that we regard 'matter', 'mind' and 'meaning' as indivisible, just as the idea of 'magnet' indivisibly consists of north and south poles and the magnetic field (discussed in Dossey). This perhaps relates to the Möbius strip model of consciousness, demonstrating the inside becoming the outside, and the outside the inside.

REMARKS ON THEORY AND EXPERIENCES

HENRI BERGSON, A NOW LARGELY FORGOTTEN philosopher of human consciousness, whose insights early in the 20thC are now beginning to be rediscovered by researchers of consciousness, didn't quite but inferred, and C.G. Jung actually stated, that "Not only is [the psyche] the condition of all metaphysical reality, it *is* that reality." Here Jung's Archetypes should be noted, for he was at pains to describe them as more than personal. They are skeletal psychic structures at birth, then filled in individually by those who acquire experiences relevant to them. A simple and near universal example is a man's experience of the feminine, mediated usually by his mother, and perhaps a sister, who thus form his foundational experience of femininity.

It has been opined that Jung was not quite stating, what I believe Swedenborg did (though I am not familiar enough with the latter's works to know precisely) that our deep consciousness *is* our connexion to the divine, the Way. Others have suggested similarly, that the route to the divine is within us: "That of God ..." as the Quakers say. Additionally I say, with Mendelssohn and many others, that words are imprecise, and can mislead, but sounds, music, speak more finely, and cannot ever speak anything but truth: this, with good intentions, cannot be other than healing, therefore close to the divine.

Dr Eben Alexander's extraordinary NDE report, just to single one example out, describes musical experiences:[31]

> A sound, huge and booming like a glorious chant, came down ... Then I heard a new sound: a *living* sound, like the richest, most complex, most beautiful music you've ever heard.

Note that Dr Alexander was adopted, as was Sharry Edwards, an exceptional person who suffered childhood trauma. Sometimes adoption, or early parental loss of other kinds, seem to be components of extraordinary personal development. As another example, J.S. Bach lost his parents when he was ten.

---

31   Alexander 2012

Helen Greaves, channelling the deceased Frances Banks,[32] notes music: A being of light came to conduct a very loving person to her appropriate 'level' (above the 'Halls of Learning').

> Then the Light grew stronger about them and there was a 'feeling' of music. ... [Negative emotions] can actually be felt and sometimes 'heard' as a low warning, drumming, rather like a wasp's buzzing.

Note the parallel with Sharry Edwards.[33]

Francisco Xavier in Brazil channelled the spirit Andre Luiz, who notes profoundly affecting music in the 'Field of Music' (his phrase). Xavier went on to channel many books about life on the other side, and he became a kind of national treasure.

ASPECTS OF TUNING

FINALLY WE RETURN TO the beginning of this paper. In a sense we have been discussing tuning all along.   "an adaptive influence or state of adaptation" could refer to the resonating body/mind system coupled with planetary vibrations.   We have hopefully "become attuned or receptive" to the concepts linked together in this somewhat rapid review of disparate ideas and information.

A short look at some properties of sound will finish this paper, in order to gain a clear idea of how the power of

---

32   Greaves, 1969
33   See p.42 in Ch..2

resonance may be affected by the tuning systems adopted. We should bear in mind that overtone properties function with all forms of vibration: thus an electrical system can resonate in 'chords' precisely as can a mechanical one.

Music tunings may be precisely 'attuned' to vibratory naturalness, what the universe does without interference from us, or not. Natural tunings (there are variations, not gone into here) represented here as Modal systems, were put down with the advent of the diatonic system of dovetailed keys, which require some adjustments from acoustic normalities in order to facilitate the typical moves from one key to another in the course of a work. This is known as equal temperament.

Different levels of resonance are obtained from the two systems. In the equal temperament system the harmonics from any note will not match exactly any other note in vibration rate (Hz) with the exception of octaves. The fifth and fourth, and to a lesser extent the third (5th harmonic), will be sufficiently close to become entrained, or at least acceptable to the ear. After that, the flat 7th harmonic and decreasing energy make it extremely unlikely that the 7th and further harmonics will be felt (or heard) on a piano normally tuned. But of course that is what is required of the equal tempered system, to be equally a compromise from all notes.

By contrast the Overtone system, built on the natural overtones, demonstrates perfectly the requirements of a modal system, eschewing modulation. Unlike the tempered scale all notes will resonate easily from the point of view of the tonic, or 'final' as it is called with respect to modal structures, on which the scale has been erected. For example take C as the fundamental at 7.8Hz: that is, all are exact pitches of the overtone sequence from C, 8th to 16th, except the 15th, or octaves of those. Part of the sequence on the D of the C sequence (*not* retuned as a parallel scale) can be an illustration. The consequence will be a reduced power of resonance compared to the resonances with the C system, whatever note is being played. Thus everything tends to refer back to the final, as it should in a mode.

This is surely what Iégor Reznikoff meant when he talked about the remarkable effects of pure sound. Since the resonating systems in the body have not been subjected to artificial temperament, it seems reasonable to suppose that, having chosen the 'correct' final, projecting tones in pure intonation will have a stronger effect because they will more readily resonate with each other and with the auditor.

However, what is the 'correct' final? The answer to this is by no means clear. We may recall Goldman's observation that different sound healers obtained appropriate effects on similar problems with dissimilar sound pitches, and his deduction concerning *intention* (Goldman: 20). This concept was picked up by the present author, but without wishing to retract anything already stated, it needs to be said that nothing has been offered here concerning the limits of action of *intention*. Someone may have researched the topic, or will.

What can be suggested out of information presented in this paper is that, in the transformation from sound to the electro-magnetic realm, several possible routes in the body were noted. When toning oneself, it becomes clear very soon that a range of pitches low to high up the body are usually required to cause the various parts to resonate. For example a medium pitch is required to resonate the chest area, whereas a high(er) pitch is needed for the head (I am deliberately not suggesting exact pitches). Thus, if we discuss the possibility of transduction via melanin or neuromelanin to produce light energy, one person may be achieving this by toning the head, thus reverberating the pineal, and another may be resonating the chest, thus agitating the melanin in the heart (Tomatis asserted that it is the heart that produces the light). This whole area is fraught with uncertainty. It is though, the arena of pragmatism: note that we have been pragmatically using electricity for more than a century, without complete understanding of it minutely.

Finally, from a curious little book by Hans Cousto, who subjected various planetary and astronomical attributes to the kind of calculation that Kepler employed in Harmonia Mundi, we see that the pitch representing one earth day is 194Hz, a slightly flat G in standard tuning, G# in the Overtone scale matched to the ubiquitous 7.8Hz as C. The tone for one year is 136Hz, a slightly flat C# in standard pitch, C¾# in the other. And the sun tone is 126Hz, B¼# in standard, a slightly sharp C in the overtone scale (Cousto). We may note that the pitch for whole body vibration established by Bentov (375Hz) is a flattish G in both systems, and so the pitches for cells and their components are flattish Cs.

The reader may make of that whatever is desired: for me it points to the interrelationship of all things, and the pervasive action of resonance in the universe.

Appendix 3. Three composers muse on life and Western art music:

Where to, and how? New music today

JB (John Burke):[1] IN OTHER WORDS: what now for serious music in the 21st century? Here in North America (I'm in Vancouver, so perhaps I reflect a 'west coast' bias) spirit, healing, consciousness as they relate to music—whose time has surely come—is pretty much the domain of traditional devotional/liturgical and new age music as well as the borrowings and blendings of world music. Classical music, certainly contemporary music, on the other hand is for the most part still the preserve of old paradigm thinking with its anachronistic Faustian politics, and dualistic, Marxist/ materialist world view. Gratuitous shock-of-the-new may have passed but the sardonic surfaces of postmodernist nihilism aren't much of an improvement.[2]

I am very interested in hearing from European composers about any stirrings in their world in the direction of merging the more radical achievements of 20th century new music with the aspirations of authentic transpersonal, shamanic or energy healing modes of transformation. I mean, something beyond the eastern European holy minimalist school, which is perfectly

---

[1]   Unexpectedly died in early 2020.

[2]   'The horror underlying existence in our time is that we no longer believe the true to be the good.' Jonathan Harvey *In Quest of Spirit*.

fine, of course. More, say, along the lines of a fusion of Sai Baba and Xenakis, if you'll forgive the impertinence!

CJ (Clement Jewitt): Sounds similar to the situation here, although, the work of Jonathan Harvey and others duly noted, I perceive a trend among contemporary composers who wish to avoid the unfeeling hegemony of the heirs of post-Schoenbergian dialectics specifically in order to grasp elusive feelings of soul and spirit, of tending to work modally or in some version of the diatonic tradition (eg Gia Kancheli from Georgia) or to borrow from other cultures (eg Alan Hovhaness your side of the pond, and several around Europe, including myself to a small extent).

One who is actively seeking to reconcile the extremes of the intellectual approach with the feeling tones of tradition (if that's the dichotomy) without middle-of-the-road compromise is the Estonian composer Erkki-Sven Tüür, though I don't think he's seeking any shamanic goal. Another composer whose works I warm to is also Estonian, Peteris Vasks, and his works do seem to have the glow of inwardness about them.

The warmth is empathic feeling. I have to confess to a personal difficulty with separating the perception of emotion from perceiving specifically spiritual emanations from music, which is my shorthand for what you describe as "authentic transpersonal, shamanic or energy healing modes".

MS (Maxwell Steer): I agree. Its like the church telling you that Christ loves you—it means nothing unless a member of that body actually realizes it in your experience.

JB: Agreed… For myself, I have been trying to do both—to the ire of some.

MS: I grew up in the Glock era of Radio 3 when you absolutely couldn't get airtime unless you were a serialist, and the more rebarbative the better. But I guess P. Maxwell Davies's evolution is exemplary, from his first, much admired, *O Magnum Mysterium* (which I thought the Emperor's new underpants) to his later symphonic music.

Have you, John, ever come across Easerley Blackwood who is, according to the web, Professor of Music at Chicago U? In the 60s/70s he used to give occasional recitals of 'second Viennese' music on Radio 3 that were electrifying; playing Webern so that rhythms were absolutely alive and newly minted. By the same token I've never heard anyone who could make Boulez *et al* sound as musical as Phyllis Bryn-Julson—her ability to marry the extremities of her range timbrelly is unsurpassed by any other singer I've heard[3]

What is extraordinary to me was the remarkable symbiotic relationship between the totalitarianism of Communism and the atonalitarianism of Serialism. The fall of the Wall was absolutely synchronous with the last gasp of a tottering

---

[3]   At that time Maxwell had not heard Wendy Nieper: see Bk.1

movement—which people like Schnittke (for whom I carry a big torch) had done so much to dislodge.

CJ: There is a group of young(ish) French composers who have emerged from under the shadow of Boulez, who may be described as post-spectralists, working with modernist procedures and spectralism as just parts of the compositional toolbox, which is the way it should be. They are in their individual ways putting melody back into the discourse, sometimes using stepwise movement which avoids being heard as diatonic by the use of intervals from higher up the harmonic series.

Here we are maybe back with notions already aired on the French character, a concern with *la ligne* which perhaps traces back through Debussy to 19ᵗʰ century opera and older French traditions. I will mention Philippe Hurel, Philippe Leroux and Thierry Blondeau (a truly beautiful clarinet quintet by the latter). I don't yet know whether as a group their music has the properties John inquires after.

JB: It would seem Grisey for his part was strenuously opposed to any extrasonic narratives around music (crudely paraphrased from a program note of a piece recently performed here: 'we're musicians pure and simple ... we're not about musical astrology, musical acupuncture, musical tarot, blah, blah, etc...'). Physics, pure and simple, evidently. But that's fine. I feel the sudden vehement emergence of abstraction in the arts at the beginning of the 20th century was an intuitive urge to return the arts to a place of healing energies in contrast to the bourgeois sentimental social function and storybook narratives of the previous century. I don't think that the West at that time was ready for it, but now with awareness of acupuncture, fengshui, healing touch, etc now virtually mainstream perhaps something new can come in.[4] Xenakis seemed to have a wild pythagorean purity about him, but he was after all a Marxist.

The Labyrinth

JB: FOR MYSELF, I'M WRITING MUSIC to accompany the walking of the Chartres labyrinth, a contemplative practice that has enjoyed a considerable revival beginning in San Francisco's Grace Cathedral and now widespread in the US. The music usually heard in this context again tends to be traditional devotional or new age; my approach will be to use the language of contemporary music in an innovative and appropriate way.

CJ: I'm very interested to hear about this. Of course the Chartres labyrinth is above ground, unlike its ancient world models. I came across a remark recently, whose authenticity I have yet to establish, to the effect that in the ancient world, Crete for example, there was a tradition of chanting while walking the labyrinth (in the dark), changing the note as you turned back on yourself down the adjacent passage, so that you

---

[4]   the American Medical Association now recognizes acupuncture—
homeopathy will no doubt take some time.

could keep some count of where you were: the implication being that part of the purpose was to submit to the transforming pressures of darkness, which links this in my mind with the 'incubation' interests of the Pythagoreans and others, whereby initiates spent time in a dark cave, that leading to transformations.

The detail goes like this: the (aboriginal?) Minotaur labyrinth at Crete[5] had seven loop passages to the eighth position, the middle. If toned from C to C, entry is at E, moving down through D to C, then jumping to F, then another jump to B, followed by A and G, with a final jump to C, the octave, which may be seen as representing the goal of a full descent into the unconscious, the Minotaur then standing for the unknown and therefore fear inspiring contents.

And perhaps musically we also have there a model of the tetrachords.[6]

JB: Fantastic... ancient corroboration of the intimate relation-ship of music with the labyrinth geometry, which seems to be inescapable when one starts working with the latter as a living ritual. Seemingly labyrinths have a different connotation to North Americans than to Europeans, to whom it is an obscure part of ancient or ecclesiastical history. Over here

---

[5] Not the so called 'Palace' at Knossos, but the curved unicursal form appearing on Cretan coins and built on or in the ground in Scandinavia and elsewhere.

[6] CDEF, GABC. Other interval sequences could be substituted, such as the ancient Greek.

it's more like a crop circle… I see it as a non-concert situation that is a perfect laboratory for working with the subconscious minds of the participants, and I'm trying to do this in a homeopathic way. By that I mean to use music (in this case for string quartet) as a carrier wave for a transpersonal intention that is empowered by and embodies the essence of the extraordinary journey of Western music. Naturally this is dependent more on the soul work of the composer than what is normally talked about in the conservatories, although it certainly includes the latter. In any case my recent experiences have convinced me that there is an extraordinary alchemy possible when sacred music and sacred geometry meet at the labyrinth.

The View from the Edge

JB: THE EASTERN ORTHODOX TRADITION and its contemporary musical emanations certainly have offered an impressive 'outsider' response to the stranglehold we seem unhappy with. In my own way I have felt the need and possibility of using quasi-tonal materials partly to get the listener to the first stage of attending to a deeper transmission. But more than that, the psycho-acoustic treasure known as the major/minor triad is not to be dismissed lightly. Despite Boulez…

I have a pet 'outsider' theory vis-a-vis 20th century music, sufficiently occult even for Colin Wilson, that posits Mahler/ Schoenberg as the shadow response/manifestations of what I see as Wagner's patriarchal psychosis about the evolutionary betrayal of the feminine healing energy in music (Wagner being my theoretical crisis point of the 1000 year trajectory of Western music) that expressed itself in his odious antisemitism, but which I dare say was not quite what it seemed (Wagner in the real world needed and honoured Jews, and they, especially the conductor Levi, revered him). In other words, perhaps the 'Jew in Music' wasn't really the issue for Wagner: it was what he wasn't honouring as an insecure, over-the-top Teutonic patriarch vis-a-vis his own anima. [Ah, to be Jung again]

Wagner himself, great artist that he was, intuited the shadow dilemma and responded, however gropingly, hopefully, with the Grail legend and his unrealized Siddhartha-themed stage work. The torch then passed to the great outsiders of the 20th century, Schoenberg (via Mahler) and Stravinsky—the wild-eyed desert mystic and the Siberian shaman—to bring forth a new dispensation, which of course they did, albeit briefly, in the riot-provoking visionary works of c.1912.

A Jew and a Russian—precisely the two outsider ethnicities that subsequently spoke to Hitler's shadow issues. The remarked-upon effeminacy of Wagner and the new revelations about the 'hidden Hitler' and his early demimondaine activities in the underground gay scene in Vienna bear some looking into.

MS: But this is surely to criticise Wagner for his merits! All male creators have to have an 'abnormally' feminine temperament otherwise they would be as insensitive to the current of the spirit as most men! I think too that a certain naivety is very helpful to a composer because if someone hasn't been taught The Best Way To Do It they're quite likely to discover something authentically person-al—which is often what tips the scales.

I saw a tv documentary recently about this 'hidden Hitler'. It was no big deal: he was just a young drifter looking for a role in the world, poking his nose (and I doubt that it was anything more!) into various lifestyles. According to this documentary, the thing that changed his 'luck' was when by chance he gave an impromptu speech about Jews in a beer cellar. Hitler was electrified by the response because in touching a nerve that evening he realised he had discovered a source of personal power. And the sequel is all too well known.

I'm afraid I have very little affection for germanic music between Weber/Brahms and Berg/Webern, so I see the real banner carriers for the spiritual essence of 'preconceived music' as Debussy and Stravinsky followed by Janàček, whose true position as a 'sleeping Bohemian knight' emerging from under the hill is one of the most resonant of the 20th century. Given the power of that myth it is no surprise for me to watch two other Slavs slowly unfold their true stature in the century after their deaths, Szymanowski and Martinù. It was really due to

Mackerras that Janáček found a foothold in the psyche of the British musical public, and if Szymanowski does likewise it will be due to Rattle.

CJ: Thinking of myth, the 20th century new music pre-occupation/fascination with percussion, read conventionally as borrowings from the exotic and/or subversion of traditional focus on pitch and line—the pursuit of colour—may be also (or more deeply considered, fundamentally) a search for the repressed feminine, something chthonic, a reconnection with earth, the ground hugging snake as ancient feminine symbol—with menstrual blood as archetypal generative, watering the earth—transformed into the reviled and feared dragon/devil by masculinised Christianity. Now percussion seeds a return to the earth via reversing that path, symbolised by sounds redolent of thunder, earthquakes, waterfalls. Visiting my brother in Uganda some years ago I noticed how often it was the women at ordinary collective events who spontaneously produced drums. Like cooking, day-to-day celebration of the sounds of the earth(mother) seemed to be regarded as women's work, while at the prestigious ceremonies the men took over and shone heroically.

MS: The issue of the re-irruption of shamanic consciousness in the 20th century is brilliantly and, I think definitively, described in Michael Tucker's *Dreaming With Open Eyes*.[7]

---

[7] HarperCollins, 1992: now out of print I believe, but well worth reading.

JB: Alas, c.1912 the West wasn't ready for that massive infusion of radically new energy, and after the miscarriage of the Great War, both society and art eventually returned to more formalist, dominator culture values. Thus the desert mystic and the Siberian shaman become the popes of their respective orthodox domains in the '30's with *Moses und Aron* (Judaism/dodecophony) and the *Symphony of Psalms* (doctrinal Christianity/neoclassicism). But now, approaching 2012, perhaps we have a window of opportunity to pick up the lost thread once again and carry it forward to its potential fruition.

CJ: Who else but an 'outsider', not party to the power base of the ruling cabal, can find the courage to expose his/her own soul in subversion of that leviathan? Parallels with other realms of endeavour abound: many of the most profound scientific advances were initiated by workers outside the mainstream, unsupported by the gatekeeper senior figures. I take some comfort from that as, somewhat like Maxwell, I am a composer who watches purveyors of empty rhetoric gain the plaudits. Fickle fashion will in time ignore them though, if not 'the judgment of history'.

Probably the necessary orientation, as you both seem to be implying in at least some of what you write, is to consciously withdraw from active pursuit of mainstream 'career' in favour of following the soul work we have been exchanging views about, in the faith emanating from inner conviction that this is the path that will (eventually) win out, or at the least survive as part of the long lineage of the esoteric threading back through all the materialistic dominances, part of the perennial tradition perhaps, sometimes lost, apparently, but only apparently lost.[8]

MS: Or is it not a 'tradition' but a reconnection to an archetypal experience of art, which underlies everything from neolithic painting to Steve Reich? This week I read of someone saying that the guy who invented the wheel was probably an artist experimenting with shapes for his own amusement.

CJ: Yes, 'archetypal' points neatly to what underlies the persistent survival of the perennial tradition: an expression of the commonality of human authentic inner experiences.

Returning to the 'outsider' motif, a young English composer, Edward Rushton, beginning to make a public mark, who lives in his wife's native Austria, reports that in his perspective the English new music scene is relatively tolerant compared to Austria where the old *avant-guard*, ensconced in the chilly heights of 'higher' learning, still largely have a stranglehold. Consequently, as his music avoids the cerebral excesses of modernism without slipping into post-modernist knowing smirks, he is being performed here, but hardly at all in Austria.

JB: Again, the need to be an outsider from the central Euro-

---

[8]   The path of the pioneer is, though, stony and booby-trapped, as I know only too well from experiences in a former career before I took up composing.

pean tradition. Eastern Europe, Scandinavia, England, and also the Americas... Perhaps that's from where the revolution now must come. The Austro-German tradition is still too addicted to its dominator culture reference points to really see the value in anything outside of itself, unless it's an extreme detour from their art music monopoly, such as Cage, or a condescending appreciation of some musical cargo cult.

CJ: This reminds me of Rudolf Steiner's remark that it would be the English to whom would fall the task of renewing music into a more spiritually oriented state.[9] As I recall he indicated the century following as the time for that unfolding... We await ...

Were his remarks Euro-centric? I don't know, but certainly they can be interpreted as a relocating of the torch of the future away from Austro-Germany, away from the centre of Europe.

JB: It seems that we in the new world are predisposed to think of serious music outside the box, outside the social roles and proprieties—and issues of legitimacy derived from lineage —that Europeans might consider basic. Thus Ives, Cage, Partch, Feldman, Reich, Glass, etc.—figures who seem to come out of nowhere and perhaps for that reason proclaim a compelling message. It's as if in the new world there is permission or a mandate for a serious music composer to imagine the state of being that s/he wishes to impart to the

---

9   Quoted in Steiner Followers 1951

listener and work backward from that to invent whatever ways and means are needed to do the job.   My feeling is that in Europe the opposite tends to be true: one starts with the lineage, the weight of tradition, the social context (there isn't one in art music in the new world) and then one tries to steer that in new directions.

MS: Well you live there John, so you'd know. My take on it is that in Europe the high priests of high art music are ring-fenced by national cultural institutions to a degree unknown in North America. Once established, the Boulezes & Berios & Birtwistles are fairly well looked after by the national broad-casters—a phenomenon that I would imagine is unknown in North America!—and are likely to receive their fair share of the public honours bestowed on cultural figures.   But there is in general, I think, nowadays, a desperate predictability to much new art music because as public support for the conservatoire æsthetic ebbs, the discourse is increasingly underwritten by academe and thus literate values, rather than emotional ones, are the principal criteria.

In Britain there is, notoriously, almost no middle ground between metronomic music, uncompromising avant-gardism and the conservatism of an aging musical public. To judge by my 'hedgerow' teaching practice I seriously wonder whether classical music is a 'spoken language' any longer.   Our commercial radio, Classic FM, has been piling on listeners, as a result of *never* challenging its listeners ears—unlike Radio 3, whose recent expansion into World Music will, I predict, have a tremendous long-term gain for breaking down the artificial division between 'art' and 'entertainment' music.

I hazard that the difference between us and N America is that its size and capitalistic character makes the kind of intellectual thought-consensus practiced by the European music establishment impossible. You don't seem to have anything like the BBC or the RTF or the WDR to assert any cultural norm. As a result North American composers *have* to make their way in a more indifferent yet less trammeled environment.

In this regard I am wholly outside the European model, for I am a composer who never found a teacher and therefore had to work out all my values for myself – hence Music & the Psyche.[10] I have therefore always empathised strongly with the scorn of such pioneers as Ives towards the sacrosanct canon of the European tradition. As a young man I seriously thought of emigrating to the USA, but I had no contacts and finally reflected that altho I was completely unacknowledged here, at least I had a social network, whereas if I were to go I wouldn't even have that! At all events, what I have drawn from 20thC American experimentalism has been, I think, a certain quality of bloody-mindedness in keeping on with my own furrow—even tho my personal idiom isn't of that character at all.

---

[10]   See Ch.9 in Bk1

JB: My own response to all of this has been to internalize the accepted journey of Western music, from plainchant as a cathedral chorister as a child up to my encounter as an undergraduate in Montreal with the lineage of Messiaen and Boulez via several of their more accomplished students. Then, in the last decade, to take a heterodox journey into the esoteric spiritual dimension of sound, music, healing and consciousness. So for me the mission is to somehow put together the astonishing story of Western music's thousand year trajectory into an unforeseen place of power and sophistication with the sonic driving, the calling in of the helping spirits—the healing intention—of the shaman's drum. Music as medicine. I have found myself strongly drawn to people who see sound and music as a form of subtle energy—chi, prana. In fact I eventually became a Reiki master myself in pursuit of this. Susan Alexjander, Fabien Maman and Don Campbell are some of the musicians who have influenced me most in this regard.

So at this point I'm trying to locate in my own terms the mysterious nexus between the aesthetic and the energetic domains of music. I sing in a harmonic men's choir here... Overtoning, the nasal sounds of Tuvan music as in the Jew's harp, Igil, etc. Again, shamanic work—oddly, it seems the helping spirits are most suitably, practically, called in with overtones and nasal sonorities! Practical psycho-spiritual music

4

making, at least in that traditional society…

CJ: There are plenty of developing European composers who collapse early under the sheer weight of the histories we have discussed, let alone strive to marry them to ancient roots— simultaneously the new opening path. May your backs prove sturdy, and the flame of your wills bright enough for the task. You articulate the heart of our matter, John, however we individually tread the path of manifestation.

Note: the exchange above with John Burke on labyrinth lore, elaborated in discussion with him later when he visited England, lead to the writing of my article on that subject, *Labyrinth: myth, meaning and symbol*. Contact me for a copy, CJ.

Bibliography

50 years Bauhaus: German exhibition. Royal Academy of Arts, 1968

Abram, David 1996. *The Spell of the Sensuous: Perception and language in a more-than-human world.* Random House

Akimov, AA & GI Shipov.(i) 1996. *Consciousness, physics of torsion fields, and torsion technologies.* Soznanie I Fizicheskaya Realnost, v1(1-2), 66-72. *English digest: Consciousness and physical reality, pp26-7*

Akimov, AA & GI Shipov.(ii) 1996. *Torsion fields and experimental evidence.* Sozn.Fiz.Real, v1(3), 28-43. *Eng. digest pp28-9*

Alexander, Eben 2012. *Proof of Heaven: A neurosurgeon's journey into the afterlife.* Piatkus.

Bakker, Karen 2022. The Sounds of Life: How digital technology is bringing us closer to the worlds of animals and plants. Princeton U.P. Oxford.

Bastin, Ted. *A clash of paradigms in physics.* IN *The encyclopaedia of ignorance, p120*

Bauhaus photography 1985. MIT P.

Bentov, Itzhak 1978. *Stalking the Wild Pendulum: On the mechanics of consci-ousness.* Wildwood Hse

Berendt, Joachim-Ernst 1988. *Nada Brahma, the World is Sound: Music and the landscape of consciousness.* East-West Publications.

Blacking, John 1976. *How Musical is Man.* Faber and Faber

Bonny, Helen L. & Louis M Savary. *Rev ed.*1990 *Music and your mind: listening with a new consciousness.* Station Hill Press

Cabinet Office 1976. *Future World Trends.* HMSO

Campbell, Don G. 1992 *Introduction to the musical brain.* MMB Music

Casson, John 2004. *Drama, Psychotherapy and Psychosis: Dramatherapy and psychodrama with people who hear voices.* Brunner-Routledge

Cottrell, *Sir* Alan 1977 *Emergent properties of complex systems.* IN The encyclo-paedia of ignorance, *p133.*

Cousto, Hans. 1988 *The Cosmic Octave: Origin of harmony.* Life Rhythm

Cymatics. https://cymascope.com *and* www.cymatics.co.uk

Daniélou, Alain 1995. *Music and the Power of Sound.* Inner Traditions. Orig. publ. as *Introduction to the Study of Musical Scales,* 1943.

Dennett, Daniel C. 1992 *Consciousness explained. Viking*

Deva, B. Chaitanya 1981. *The Music of India: A scientific study.* Munshiram Manoharlal Pvt.

Devereux, Paul 2001. *Stone Age Soundtracks: The acoustic archaeology of ancient sites.* Vega

Devereux, Paul et.al., eds 2008 - . *Time & Mind: The journal of archaeology, consciousness and culture.* Berg

Dona, Mariangela 1977. *Forma pittorica e forma musicale in Paul Klee.* IN *Gatti Festscrift,* 1977

Dossey, Larry 1993. *Healing Breakthroughs: How your attitudes and beliefs can affect your health.* Piatkus

Eliade, Mircea 1964. *Shamanism: Archaic techniques of ecstasy.* (Bollingen series LXXVI). Rev & enlarged from the French, 1951

Encyclopaedia of ignorance: everything you ever wanted to know about the unknown. 1977 Ronald Duncan & Miranda Weston-Smith, eds. Pergamon Press

Farmer, John D & Geraldine Weiss 1971. *Concepts of the Bauhaus: the Busch-   Reisinger Museum Collection.* B-R Museum, Harvard U.

Franciscono, Marcel 1971. *Walter Gropius and the creation of the Bauhaus in Weimar.* U Illinois P.

Gilliam, Bryan (ed) 1994. *Music and performance during the Weimar Republic.* Cambridge UP.Goldman, Jonathon 1996. *Healing Sounds: The power of harmonics.* rev.ed. Thorsons

Gladzewski, *Rev.* Andrew. 1951 *The music of crystals, plants and human beings.* Radio perception, Sept.1951, 15-37

Goldman, Jonathan 1996. *Healing Sounds: The power of harmonics.* Rev. ed. Thorsons

Greaves, Helen 1969. *Testimony of Light: An extraordinary message of life after death.* Rider.

Harman, Alec 1962. *Man and his Music: The story of musical experience in the West.* Part 1: *Mediaeval and Early Renaissance Music.* Barrie & Jenkins

Harvey, Jonathan 1999. *In Quest of Spirit: Thoughts on music.* U. California Press

Hawkins, David R. 1995(2012) *Power vs Force: The hidden determinants of human behavior;* - 2001. *The Eye of the I: From which nothing is hidden;* - 2003. *I: Reality and subjectivity.* Hay House

Head, Raymond 2012. Gustav Holst and India. Sky Dance Press

Hill, Gareth S. 1992. *Masculine and Feminine: The natural flow of opposites in the psyche.* Shambhala

Ho, Mae-Wan & Fritz-Albert Popp 1991. *On the coherent lightness of being.* Caduceus No13, Spring *1991, pp28-31*

Itten, Johannes 1975. *Design and form: the Basic course at the Bauhaus.* rev. ed. Thames & Hudson

Jenny, Hans 2001. *Cymatics: A study of wave phenomena and vibration.* English ed. Macromedia publishing

Jung, Carl Gustav CW9i (Collected Works vol.9i). *The Archetypes and the Collective Unconscious*

Jung, C. G. CW10. *Civilisation in Transition.*

Jung, C.G. *Letters V.1*

Koestler, Arthur. 1971 *Beyond reductionism; new perspectives in the life sciences.* Houghton Mifflin

Khayaal Theatre Company www.khayaal.co.uk

Klemm, Eberhardt 1989. *Stefan Wolpe: ein fast vergessener Berliner Komponist.* Henschel.

Korotkov, KG.1996 *Experimental study of activity of human consciousness after biological death.* Sozn.Fiz.Real. v1(1-2), 103-108. *Eng. digest p46*

Kroher, Ekkehart 1975. *In Memory of an Angel* [record sleeve]

Lang, Rose-Carol Washton 1980. *Kandinsky: the development of an abstract style.*

Laszlo, Ervin 1997. *3rd Millenium: The challenge and the vision: The Club of Budapest report on creative paths of human evolution.* Gaia Books

Laszlo, Ervin 1997. *Life - a dance through the zero-field.* Caduceus No38 Winter 97, pp.15-18,78.

Lee, Brian 1997. *Symbiosis: Perfecting the art of relaxation.* Caduceus No38, Winter 97, p55

Leeds, Joshua 1995. *Frequency Medicine for the 21st Century: A sympathetic vibration.* Caduceus No28 Autumn 95, 27-30

Lorimer, David. 1990 *Whole in one: the near death experience and the ethic of interconnectedness.* Arcana

Lorimer, David & Robinson, Oliver eds. 2010. *A New Renaissance: Transforming science, spirit and society.* Floris Bks

Loupe, Laurence 1987. *Voir, danser, creer: la danse au Bauhaus. IN* Marsyas, V. 3-4, Dec 87.

McClellan, Randall 1991. *The healing forces of music: history, theory and practice.* Harper Collins

McGilchrist, Iain 2009. *The Master and his Emissary: The divided brain and the making of the Western world.* Yale.

McIntosh, Solveig 2005. *Hidden Faces of Ancient Indian Song.* Ashgate

Maman, Fabien. 1997 *The role of music in the twenty first century.* Book 1 of *From star to cell: a sound structure for the twenty first century.* Tamado Press

Mansfield, Victor. 1997 *An astrophysicist's sympathetic and critical review of astrology, http://lightlink.com/vic/astrol.html*

Meadows, Dennis L. 1974 *The Limits to Growth: A report for The Club of Rome's Project on the Predicament of Mankind.* Potomac 8 Pan Books. First pub 1972

Mithen, Steven 2005. *The Singing Neanderthals: The origins of music, language, mind and body.* Weidenfeld & Nicolson

Muyle, Jan 1989. *De affiniteit van Oskar Schlemmer met muziek, toneel, en ballet.* IN Adem: *3 maandelijks tijdschrift voor musikalischen Volkskunde,* XXV / 1, 89

Neher, Andrew 1962. *A Physiological Explanation of Unusual Behaviour in Ceremonies Involving Drums.* Human Biology Vol.34 No.2 (151-160)

Neumann, Eckhard (ed) 1970. *Bauhaus and Bauhaus people: Personal opinions and recollections.* Van Nostrand Reinhold.

Noel-Baker, Philip 1978. *The worst kind of poverty: Poverty of mind. IN* UNESCO 1978

Old Hall MS. British Library, *Add MS 57950*

Peccei, Aurelio 1978. *Man, an abandoned world. IN* UNESCO 1978 Mithen, Steven 2005. *The Singing Neanderthals: The origins of music, language, mind and body.* Weidenfeld & Nicolson

Penrose, Roger. 1994 *Shadows of the mind: a search for the missing science of consciousness.* Reviewed in Searle 1997.

Petche, Hellmuth *et al. 1993. EEG coherence and musical thinking.* Music perception. v11(2), 117-151   *(Winter 1993)*

Pinker, Steven 1997. *How the Mind Works.* Norton

Polanyi, Michael. 1958 *Personal Knowledge: Towards a post critical philosophy.* Routledge & Kegan Paul

Positive News www.positivenews.org.uk

Power of Hope *www.powerofhope.org*

Rauscher, Frances et.al. 1993. *Music and Spatial Task Performance. Nature Vol. 365, 14th October*

Reznikoff, Iegor 1994. *Therapy of Pure Sound: Interview.* Caduceus No23, Summer 94, 16-18

Robinson, J. Bradford. *Jazz reception in Weimar Germany: in search of a shimmy figure.* IN Gilliam, Bryan, (ed.) 1994

Rosenthal, Erwin 1971. *Contemporary art in the light of history.* Lund Humphries

Roters, Eberhard 1969. *Painters of the Bauhaus.* Praeger.

Rowell, Lewis 1983. *Thinking About Music: an introduction to the philosophy of music.* University of Massachusetts Press.

Sardar, Ziauddin & Iwona Abrams 1998. *Chaos for Beginners.* Icon Books.

Schlain, Leonard 1998. *The Alphabet versus the Goddess: Male words & Female Images.* Allen Lane, Penguin

Schlemmer, Oskar 1971. *Man: teaching notes from the Bauhaus.* Lund Humphries.

Schlemmer, Oskar, Laszlo Moholy-Nagy & Molnar Farkas 1979. *The Theater of the Bauhaus.* Eyre Methuen.

Schroeder-Sheker, Therese 1994. *Music for the Dying.* Caduceus No23, Summer 94, 24-27

Searle, John R. 1997 *The mystery of consciousness.* Granta Books

Shushan, Gregory 2022. *The Next World: Extraordinary experiences of the afterlife.* White Crow Books

Skelton, Geoffrey 1977. *Paul Hindemith: the man behind the music.* Gollancz.

Stuckenschmidt, Hans Heinz 1985. *Musik am Bauhaus*. IN *Vom klang der Bilder - Die Musiek in der Kunst der 20 jahrhundert*. [Exhibition catalogue] Prestel.

Targ, Russell & K. Harary. 1984 *The mind race: understanding and using psychic abilities*. Random House

Tilly, Margaret. https://alchemicalcoffins.tumblr.com/post/99284222842/carl-jung-and-music-therapy-margaret-tilly-a

Tomatis, Alfred 1992. *The Conscious Ear: My life of transformation through listening*. Station Hill Press

UNESCO 1978. *What kind of world are we leaving our children?* Amadou-Mahtar M'Bow & others

Virilio, Paul 2003. *Art and Fear*. Athlone Press

Voeikov, VL. 1996 *On the structure/energy specificity of the living state*. Sozn.Fiz.Real. v1(4), 61-65. *Eng. digest p53*

Watson, Lyall. 1974 *Supernature: A natural history of the supernatural*. Coronet Books

Wilson Schaef, Anne 1992. *Beyond Therapy, Beyond Science: A new model for healing the whole person*. Harper Collins

Wilson, William. 1997 *Resonance and the cranial system*. Therapeutic pulse

Wingler, Hans M. 1975. *The Bauhaus, Weimar, Dessau, Berlin, Chicago*, 3rd rev ed. MIT P. (orig. publ. as *Das Bauhaus*, 1962). Definitive work

Woolger, Roger. 1990 *Other Lives, Other Selves*. Aquarian Press

Zuckerkandl, Victor 1973. *Man the Musician*. (Sound & symbol, Vol 2). Princeton UP

Index of Names